Thank You Lord Jesus

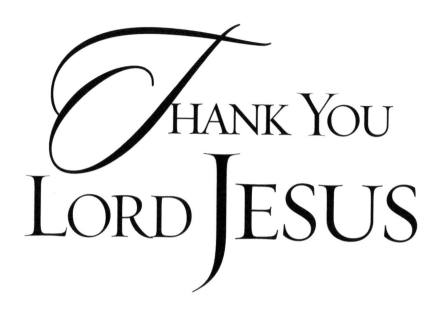

THANK YOU LORD JESUS

KIM STANLEY

CREATION HOUSE

THANK YOU, LORD JESUS by Kim Stanley
Published by Creation House
A Strang Company
600 Rinehart Road
Lake Mary, Florida 32746
www.creationhouse.com

Author photo by Herb Bias

Cover design by Jamey Bartenhagen

Author's note: some names have been changed to protect
identities.

Library of Congress Control Number: 2007926960
International Standard Book Number: 978-1-59979-216-3

First Edition

07 08 09 10 11 — 987654321

Printed in the United States of America

*T*his book is dedicated to Christopher, my angel who is in heaven, and Christian, my angel here on earth. I thought I knew what love was, but I had no clue until you both came into my life. My love for you is beyond what words can describe. Mommy loves you both.

ACKNOWLEDGMENTS

*F*IRST I WANT to thank the true author of this book, our Lord and Savior, Jesus Christ, for without Him there would be no Kim Stanley. I am a true witness of your love, grace, and mercy; because of this I thank You, Lord Jesus.

I want to thank my best friend, my confidante, and the wind beneath my wings—my mother, Bettye Stanley Hines. I learned how to love you, my mother, by watching you love your mother, and I learned how to be a mother by living as your daughter. I thank you and I love you!

And I have to thank the loves of my life—my angels, Christopher and Christian. I love you so much, Christian, there are no words to express the depth of my love for you. The unconditional love and support you give to Mommy is something I can never forget, and I could never live without your love. Kim is my name, but you gave me one that can never compare—Mommy. Christian, I love you with every ounce of my being and to the depths of my soul. Thank you for allowing me to give you what your older brother taught me in such a small amount of time—the true power and meaning of love. Christian, never forget that even when you're fifty years old, you will always be my baby.

Cynthia, it's an honor to be your big sister. Thank you for all the sacrifices you endure for me. Always remember to let go and let God do what He wants with you.

Sheldon, my time with you has given me some things I require: lessons on life, love, and relationships. Thank you, Professor Ferguson.

To my pastor and church family, Pastor Otis Moss Jr. and Olivet Institutional Baptist Church, thank you for your love and support throughout the years. I couldn't and wouldn't have made it without all of you. A special thanks goes to my personal Kinko's department— Dobbie Miller. I love you all!

To every doctor, nursing assistant, and medical staff member who has cared for me the past twenty years, thank you for never allowing me to be another chart number, but an individual with feelings and fears. Your medical expertise is one of the many reasons I'm still here.

To my family and friends, thanks for keeping me grounded and for being my biggest fans. To all my fans from my radio career who never forgot me, thank you for keeping me in their prayers. To all my naysayers, doubters, and haters, thank you. You're some of the many reasons my knees stay on the ground in prayer.

CONTENTS

INTRODUCTION

⁓

*T*HANK YOU, LORD JESUS is a title, but more than a title, it is a testimony. It is a testimony of struggles, strengths, and strides. It is an autobiographical testament of a remarkable young woman—one who would not surrender on the battlefields of human stress, strain, cancer, and a tragic accident which resulted in the death of her firstborn and left her in a coma for several days. Kim Stanley has taken critical pieces of her life's journey and given us a redemptive tapestry of God's amazing grace.

I have known Kim since her teenage years and have prayed with her and her family through what could easily be described as "dangers, toils, and snares." What I have seen again and again is ability, integrity, faith, hope, love, and growth. Every challenge has deepened her faith in

God. Kim keeps coming back with renewed commitment as a disciple of Jesus Christ. Her beloved mother, Betty Hines, sister, stepfather, and others planted around her a beautiful garden of intercessory prayers. When Kim was in a coma, her mother kept tape recordings of beautiful music at her bedside, reinforcing Dr. Deforia Lane's thesis that certain types of music can be great medicine in therapy, care, and recovery.

I recommend this book to everyone, and especially young adults who hunger for the highway of health, healing, and wholeness.

—THE REVEREND DR. OTIS MOSS JR.
PASTOR, OLIVET INSTITUTIONAL BAPTIST CHURCH

CHAPTER I

My Roots

THE QUIET, SUBDUED woman was pregnant, and she didn't want to keep her baby. There was a deacon in her church in Cleveland who helped her whenever things were rough, and she knew that he and his wife couldn't have children. Thus, when she gave birth to a baby boy on November 15, 1947, she gave him to the deacon and his wife, Julius and Mattie Stanley. The happy couple named him after the deacon, calling him Julius L. Stanley, Jr. Meanwhile, down south in the rural area of Jonestown,

Mississippi, a proud, strong woman gave birth to a baby girl on April 13, 1946, and named her Bettye Fisher.

Bettye was the eleventh of fifteen children born to Mack and Ida Fisher. Life in the Deep South wasn't easy in the 1940s, and blacks were mistreated on a daily basis. One day a group of white men came in the middle of the night and took Mack away. They used him as a guinea pig to test a new drug that didn't work, and he died when Bettye was only seven years old. Her mother was left to raise fourteen children alone, while Bettye's older brother Mack went away to the service and saved his money. In 1959 he came and took his mother, brothers, and sisters off the plantation where they lived. They relocated up north in Cleveland, Ohio.

One day while Bettye was relaxing on the couch, Ida asked her to go stop the group of boys who were picking a fight with her younger brother Sam. Fourteen-year-old Bettye jumped off the couch, ran down two flights of stairs to the boys who were picking on her brother, and proceeded to beat them up individually. Julius, who was thirteen, was sitting on his bike watching the scene and laughing at his friends who were being punished by, as he says, "This high-yellow girl, with the prettiest green hazel eyes I'd ever seen."

When she finished beating the boys, Julius didn't think about staying. He got off his bike and started to run, but Bettye caught him and gave him a beating he never forgot. "That's when I knew I was in love with that yellow, green-eyed girl named Bettye Fisher," Julius said.

The love between Bettye and Julius started that day, and it withstood all the challenges of adolescent life. Julius went to West Tech High School and Bettye went to East High School. When he was eighteen, Julius joined the Air Force and prepared to fight in the Vietnam War, but he knew he wanted someone special to be waiting for him at home. He proposed to Bettye, the girl who had won his heart when he was thirteen, and she said yes. Julius fought in the Vietnam War and finally came home to his awaiting blushing bride. They were married on December 25, 1967.

Shortly after their marriage, Bettye gave Julius the joyous news that they were expecting their first baby. During her pregnancy she became an avid reader. She read to her unborn child and told her how she would always love her. She made the decision to dedicate her life to caring for her. Finally, on Sunday, March 28, 1971, at St. Ann's Hospital in Cleveland, Ohio, Bettye gave birth to a 6 lb. 6 oz. daughter named Kimberley Michelle Stanley. Julius almost passed out because he was so overcome with fear, anxiety, and the sight of his daughter's delivery.

MY FRIGHTENING INTRODUCTION TO ABUSE

My mother named me Kimberley Michelle because of the influence of two close relationships. Her good friend Jewel Haynes always wanted a girl and said, "If I ever had a girl, I would call her Kimberley." My mother thought it was a beautiful name. My middle name came from my mother's favorite niece, Michelle. My mother was so proud of me, and my father fell in love with my light brown eyes.

Our family first lived in an apartment on the east side of Cleveland in the St. Clair area. My father had a good job with the Phillip Morris Company, and my mother was employed by Society National Bank (now called KeyBank), where she still works. My parents saved their money and bought a house on Meadowbrook Lane in the Cleveland suburb of Warrensville Heights. They were so proud of their new home. My father went out and bought two dogs, a Black Poodle he named Quincy and a white Samonsite he called Chico.

I had everything a little girl could want. I even had a playroom with my own miniature table and tea set, and I frequently demanded that my father be my tea partner.

At that time, I looked at my father as my hero and my daddy. I believed that he could do no wrong. However, I was wrong. When my father came back from Vietnam to his bride, his spirit and demeanor were totally changed from the way he had been before he went there. He was a man my mother had never known or would ever have dreamed he could be—a Dr. Jekyll and Mr. Hyde.

One day I was playing in my playroom when I heard my father yelling at my mother. My parents always closed the door when Daddy was fussing, but this time he was yelling loudly and beating her too. My mother tried to run away from him, and I heard her scream "Stanley, stop! Leave me alone."

As I ran out and stood at the bottom of the steps, I saw a scene that I will never forget. My father had my mother's hair in one hand and hit her in the face with his other hand. She flew in the air, hit the stairs, and tumbled down, hitting the rail and landing at the bottom of the steps. When I looked at her face, all I could see was blood. Her leg was also covered with blood from hitting the rail on the staircase. When my mother looked at me and began to cry, I screamed in horror. "You killed my Mommy!"

My father looked at me and said, "Bettye, get up." My mother said nothing but sat there and cried and reached for me. She reassured me that she was OK and said

I could stop crying. When my father came down the stairs and saw all the blood, he said to my mother, "Look at what you made me do. Come on; get up. I'm taking you to the hospital."

Although we could have gone to a hospital right around the corner from where we lived, my father drove all the way to Mt. Sinai Hospital in inner-city Cleveland. As we went, my mother sat hunched over in the back seat and comforted me. When we arrived at the hospital, my father did something very cold. He pulled up to the emergency room door, told my mother that we would wait for her in the car, and said that she had better watch her mouth.

We sat in the car for a long time. I remember jumping up and looking anxiously at the door to see if Mommy was coming out, but each time it was either a doctor or a nurse. The last time I turned around quicker than usual and saw my father looking at the door too. Our eyes met and for the first time I looked at him with so much anger. "Why are you looking at like that?" he asked.

"I hate you!" I replied.

"What did you say to me?"

I said it again louder, "I hate you!"

"Why you little…" he said and raised his hand. Just then, my mother came out of nowhere, stuck her head in the car, and said the words that have protected me all the days of my life: "Stanley," she said, "you put your hands on me all the time and I take it. One day I'm not going to take it any longer. But if you ever put your hands on my baby, I'll kill you. Remember, Stanley, that's one trip to hell I'll take."

I was so happy to see my mother that I jumped up, forgetting about my father, and said, "Mommy are you OK?"

"Sweetheart," she assured me, "Mommy is just fine. Scoot over so I can sit next to you." She limped as she opened the door, and as she hopped into the back seat, I stared at her leg. It was covered in bandages with bloodstains.

"Are you going to die?" I asked her.

"Oh no," she replied, "these are called stitches."

My father looked at the wound, turned around, and started driving. I fell in my mother's arms and went to sleep. The next morning I awoke in her arms. I do not know how I got there, but I was just glad to be with my mother. I smelled the sweet, subtle smell of the baby powder aroma that brought me such security throughout my younger years of childhood.

After that incident in the hospital parking lot my mother did not leave me alone with my father. When she went to work, she left me at one of three places I came to consider my other homes: my grandmother's apartment, my Auntie Thelma's house, or my Uncle Mark's house. The man I loved so much had turned into a monster I couldn't stand. He was a traveling salesman, and whenever he went out of town, I would tell my mother, "I hope he never comes back." She always scolded me and said I should never disrespect my father. He was still my father, she explained, and the Lord would deal with him in due time.

The Influence of My Grandparents

The importance of always respecting your elders and your parents was a lesson my mother learned from her mother, Ida Fisher. I used to ask my grandmother, "Grandma, can me, you, and Mommy run away from Daddy?"

My grandmother would hug me and say, "Lord Jesus, protect my babies." Then she would say, "How about me and you running away downtown?"

We would catch the bus downtown and go to a store called Woolworth's. There we would sit in the same booth and share a hot dog, potato chips, and pop. We only got one because that's all Grandma could afford, but

I didn't know that then. I just thought she loved me so much she wanted to share my treat with me. After lunch my grandmother completed our trip with a coloring book, crayons, and a walk downtown. That meant the world to me. Being with my grandmother was an escape from the reality of home, and I love her so much for it.

One of the traditions from the South was that everyone in our family called my grandmother, Mother. I didn't like it and I wanted to change her name to Grandma. I said, "Mother, everybody calls you Mother. Is that because it's what you are, or is that your name?"

She laughed and said, "No! My name is Ida Mae, and Mother is what everybody calls me."

"But you are not my mother," I replied. "You are my grandmother. Could I call you Grandma, because Daddy's mother is my granny?"

Once again she laughed and said, "Yes. You can call me Grandma." That's when I started calling her by that name.

Another memory about my grandmother brings laughter to my heart and mind. When my mother was teaching me the dos and don'ts and rights and wrongs, we went over to my grandma's apartment. My mother rang the buzzer to gain entrance into the building, and

Grandma let us in without asking who we were. When we got to my grandmother's door, she opened it with her usual big smile, and I let go of my mother's hand to run and greet her. My mother said, "Mother, you just don't buzz people in and answer the door without asking who it is."

Grandma pulled me into the apartment, looked at my mother, and slammed the door in her face. A look of shock and amazement came over me. I couldn't believe that my grandmother slammed the door in my mother's face. As she smiled at me, we heard my mother knocking on the door saying, "Mother, why did you slam the door in my face?"

"Who is it?" my grandma asked.

At that moment I saw grandma in a whole new light. Not only was she a lady of style and dignity, but she also was a woman you should not push the wrong way. When Grandma opened the door, Mommy had a smirk on her face and said, "Mother that wasn't called for, and how are you doing?"

Grandma gave her the response I heard all my life, "I'm doing fine, thank the Lord."

My other grandparents were my father's parents, Deacon Julius and Mattie Stanley. I called my grandfather Grandpa and my grandmother Granny. My granny was an elegant lady who played the piano and had class. I was closer to my grandfather than my grandmother because he just loved me with all his heart. My granny would always say, "Kimberley, you act too much like a boy, baby. You are a lady. Always conduct yourself in a ladylike manner."

Grandpa would whisper to me, "Baby, just be who you are and have fun being you. Don't worry about Granny, she'll get over it." Then he would give me a kiss and a piece of Juicy Fruit gum. He always had a stick of gum for me when he saw me. Whether it was fresh or stale, Grandpa was always prepared for me.

I didn't spend the night at my grandparents' house very often because my granny always complained about how boyish I was and the way I tortured her cats. She loved cats and had many of them around her house. I hated cats because they were always were around and made noise—*meow, meow, meow.*

To this day I do not know my paternal grandmother. I have tried to look for her, but I have no information about her. The answers to my questions are with my father's adoptive parents, who died over ten years ago. My father never knew much because it wasn't discussed with him. I don't know if my father's mother is alive, but I do admire her and hold a special place for her in my heart. I am grateful to her because I am here today as a result of her decision to place my father in the home of Deacon Julius and Mattie Stanley. Now that I'm a mother, I understand her love.

My father's mother apparently kept a strong interest in my father's life and knew a lot about him. On March 28, 1971, my mother was nursing me in her hospital room when a woman came in and greeted her. Walking slowly to my mother's bed, she stared at me and smiled. At first my mother thought her visitor was a church member she hadn't met yet. But as the woman caressed my face with the side of her hand, she looked at my mother and said, "I don't care what anybody says, this is my granddaughter. I'm Julius's real mother."

The words left my mother shocked and speechless. My grandmother smiled at me again and walked out of the room, never to contact us again. My mother said that my father looks a lot like his mother. I can only imagine the pain she suffered as she watched from a distance and saw her son grow up, unable to kiss him, hold him, and simply love him. It would destroy my heart and being. Yet she did this and never missed a beat. I say to her, "Thank you!"

CHAPTER 2

My Family

MY MOTHER SUPPLIED everything I needed and wanted. We had a roof over our head, food to eat, and clothes and shoes to wear. My father, a traveling salesman for Phillip Morris, usually went out of town every two weeks. When he left, he limited my mother's use of the car to work purposes only. He would monitor the mileage to see if she went anywhere else.

Because we had to stay home all the time, we could not do much in the winter. However, since we lived about three streets from the city park, summer was the best. My mom had saved up her money and bought me a red wagon with a black handle, black wheels with spokes, and the words *Red Rider* on the side. She pulled me in my red wagon everywhere we went in the neighborhood and would always take me to the park. Sometimes she would pack a lunch for us to eat there. I loved to be pushed on the swings and ride the sliding board.

My father had his good side, and some days he was the best dad in the world. But he was still abusing my mother mentally in front of me and physically in private. The physical abuse was not as private as he wanted, and I always tried to help my mother by hitting and biting my father when I saw him hurting her. During those tender toddler years I became very close to my mother and drew away from my father as much as possible.

When my father went out of town, my mommy and I had the best time. She would cook my favorite dinner: fried chicken, French fries, and green beans with a tall glass of grape Kool-Aid. She might put on her favorite records by Natalie Cole and Teddy Pendergrass, turn them up loud, and sing to them. She let me do whatever I wanted to do, which was watching TV or playing with our dog Quincy. When she finished doing what needed to be done, my mother would get two books and read them to me every night. Most of the time I would fall asleep in her bed or wherever she read to me.

In the winter we would end up at my Auntie Thelma's or my Grandma's on weekdays. Auntie Thelma didn't live far from us, and I was close to her daughter, Cliffchelle. We enjoyed terrorizing her brother Leonard, especially when he was talking to girls on the phone or in the basement with his friends. Leonard's famous line was, "Cliffchelle and Kim, ya'll need to get away from me. Mom, call these crazy little girls away." My Auntie Thelma would always tell both him and us to leave each other alone.

On the weekend I would terrorize another cousin, Michelle. At that time I believed it was my duty to constantly bother Michelle. I tortured her with questions and ran in and out of her room disturbing her while she tried to sleep. I still call her by my nickname for her, "Ugly," and I still hold the title she gave me, "Brat." I love all my cousins, but Michelle is different. With her, it's a love with no definition or explanation; it's an admiration and affection that go beyond what words could ever express.

My family is the best. I couldn't compare them and never will. I wouldn't be here without them today. When I look at my uncles, I see them as father figures, especially my Uncle Al. He was my heart and my protector, and nothing anyone says about him can tarnish my love for him. The same is true for my Uncle Sam and Uncle Mack. If I didn't know any better, I would think they were my fathers because they were always there for my mother and me. My Uncle Isador is a picture of humility and has a sincere smile on his face no matter what is happening.

Uncle Isador's gracious character is also found in my Auntie Alberta and Aunt Azalee. Those women are so sincere, humble, and compassionate. Words cannot express how loving they are. My grandparents had ten girls and five boys, and my aunts vary in all forms of love. For example, you don't want to mess with my Auntie Carmella. And my aunt Lucillee and Auntie Emma keep me going with laughter. They taught me that laughter is the best medicine no matter what the situation is. All my other Aunts—Pamella, Fannie and Rosie—give love that goes beyond definition.

THE BIRTH OF MY SISTER, CYNTHIA

Although it was a little lonely at times, it was great being the only child. My main interest was reading books, and I read everything Judy Blume, my favorite childhood author, wrote. I enjoyed reading from a young age because my mother always read to me before she put me to bed at night. My fascination with reading grew to the point that I would continue reading under the bed sheets with my flashlight when she left.

One day my mother sat me down and told me that she was pregnant. My first question was if I would have a brother or a sister. My mother told me she didn't know, but in seven months I would be somebody's big sister.

Her pregnancy went well, although it did have its difficult moments when my father was mean toward her, especially verbally. He always told her he didn't want the baby because they couldn't afford it. He said they didn't need another one, but Mommy stood firm with her decision to keep her baby, even when my father would slap her or hit her.

She did well until one day when she was eight months pregnant. While she and my father were arguing, he punched her in the stomach and threw her down the stairs. I had never seen my mother in so much pain, and I was so scared for my mother. I didn't know what to do. My father left, and when he did my mother made a series of phone calls. The next thing I knew a taxi driver came to our house and took us to the greyhound bus station. As she pulled our suitcase out of the trunk, I asked my mother where we were going.

"Sweetheart," she replied, "we are going to Auntie Alberta in Chicago."

"Are we going to live there?"

"For a little while," she responded.

And that's where we stayed until my mother was close to her delivery date. I loved staying with my Auntie Alberta because she always made me laugh. She had the prettiest smile in the world, and it was always there no matter what. We finally went home to my father, who was now nice and kind and did everything to make my mother comfortable. However, I didn't trust him. I was very angry with him about hitting Mommy and the baby, and my hatred toward him grew.

On Sunday morning February 4, 1979, my mother was cooking breakfast when I suddenly heard a loud crashing sound. "Stanley, the baby is coming," my mother cried.

I ran to my mother and found her on her knees holding her stomach. After my father got her in the car and put me in the back seat, I leaned over the seat and kissed my mother on the cheek. "Mommy, please don't have the baby in the car. You are supposed to have the baby in the hospital."

My father drove the Cadillac through a couple red lights on our way to the hospital, and my Auntie Thelma was there to take me to her house. When my mother and I were separated, she was in so much pain, yet she still winked at me and blew me a kiss. I was so happy and yet so scared.

About an hour after I arrived at Auntie Thelma's house, she came into Cliffchelle's room with a big smile. "Kim," she said, "you have a baby sister."

My heart leaped for joy. Cliffchelle and I jumped on her bed, and then I ran around screaming, "I'm a big sister now!"

I was so excited I couldn't control myself. Suddenly I remembered my mother and found my Auntie Thelma in the kitchen. Running over to her, I asked, "Auntie Thelma, how's my mommy?"

My Auntie smiled and said she was doing just fine.

I smiled and found Cliffchelle, and we started screaming again. All the time we were doing this, Leonard yelled at us to stop because he was trying to get some sleep.

When my mother came home with the baby, I asked what its name was. My father had hoped for a boy, so my mother had planned to name the baby Julius after him. Since the baby was a girl, my mother talked about naming her Julie. However, I told her I didn't like that name so my mother chose the name Cynthia.

Life With Cynthia

Life changed after Cynthia was born. I was no longer the center of attention, and I had to share the spotlight. This was hard for me because I had been the only child for eight years. Cynthia was a happy baby and always had a smile on her face. She constantly kissed us baby-style, opening her mouth and gumming down on our faces with huge amounts of slobber. She became the apple of my father's eye, and he was crazy about her.

One day I overheard my father telling Cynthia how much he loved her. He couldn't imagine not ever having her, and she couldn't do any wrong in his eyes. I was jealous because I could not remember that he had ever treated me that way. When I wouldn't let Cynthia play with some of my toys, she would clap her hands together and pretend to cry. My father would rush down to see what was wrong, and he would always believe her side of the story. Then he would punish me for doing something I never did. Cynthia had my father wrapped around her finger.

The little part of a father I had before was now given to her, and I felt like I was abandoned, traded in for a better version of a child. However, as time went on I began to outgrow my need to be acknowledged by my father. I pushed him off to the side and would not allow him to hurt or bother me.

Since Mom was busy working, I started to care for Cynthia in a motherly way. Maybe because of this, she had a tendency to follow me everywhere I went, and this drove me crazy sometimes. I was a rugged tomboy, and she was a perfect, angelic lady, like our granny desired. Still, I didn't want anybody to make fun of Cynthia, and I took offense to anyone who bothered her.

Cynthia was a chunky child, or as my mother would say, a *healthy* child. Sometimes the kids on the street would tease Cynthia, and this made me angry. One time a boy was teasing Cynthia, and I tried to help her by telling her how to respond to his unkind remarks. At one point, I whispered to Cynthia and encouraged her to say, "At least my momma don't look like a pit bull dog." However, when Cynthia repeated it, she changed it to, "At least my mother looks like a pit bull dog!" When Cynthia's tormenter started laughing, she was confused. However, I was so upset that I balled up my fist and hit him in the face. After that incident I stopped telling Cynthia what to say. I just started fighting anyone who had something negative to say to my sister.

"Your sister is all you have," my mother advised. "Friends will come and go, but no one will stay with you like a sister. There is a bond between the two of you, and it's the fact that you are sisters. Don't let anyone break it." Cynthia and I are still like night and day. She is my father's twin, and I look like my mother. Yet, even though we are so different I love her deeply. No matter what, I'll always love my Cynthia.

My Decision for Christ

There are many days in life I will never forget, like the Sunday evening when I gave my life to Christ. I was nine years old, and we were at a church function—the viewing of a movie called A Stranger in the Night. It was about what was going to happen when Jesus comes back in the final resurrection. To be honest, it really scared me about what would happen to me if Jesus didn't take me back to heaven with Him.

My father was one of the ministers that night. He was called to be a minister when he was in his late teens, and he grew up being a teen minister who was known as the young electrifying minister with perfect pronunciation of words.

After the movie, I thought and thought, but I didn't make my decision out of fear, I made it out of love. I knew that I loved God with all my heart, and I wanted to give my life to Him. I remember walking down the aisle to give my life to God and saying these words: "Here I go, God. I want to be a part of Your family. Father, I hope I'm worthy enough that You will be willing to use me to do Your will...I'm Yours, Lord."

As I sat down in the chair, I looked at the crowd and saw my mother crying and rejoicing with gratefulness to the Lord. Then when I looked at my father, I saw a look on his face of such great pride that I knew I made the right decision. My heart and soul said and felt so, and the looks on my parents' faces reassured me that I did so.

CHAPTER 3

School Days

I WAS A shy, quiet student when I began elementary school, but that changed one day in Ms. June White's second grade class. A girl named Deann was playing with a toy under her desk, and I wanted to play with it too. I was so interested in the toy that I didn't hear the teacher call on me to answer a question. She called my name over and over, and finally I snapped out of my trance and yelled, "What is it woman?"

Everyone, including the teacher, turned and looked at me in amazement and shock. Ms. Black came over to me and snatched my arm. "Young lady," she said, "don't you ever speak to me in that tone."

"Why? It's not like you're my mother," I retorted, "and to be honest, you were bothering me."

She immediately sent me to the principal's office. As I prepared to leave the classroom, all the children looked at me like I was a superhero. I had done the unthinkable; I had talked back to the teacher. On my way out of the classroom, I had to pass the teacher's desk. She was sitting down, and as I walked behind her, I stuck out my tongue at her. Everyone started laughing and she said, "Kim, what did you do?"

I looked back at her and said, "You're the teacher…figure it out." The next thing I knew, she snatched my arm and dragged me down to the principal's office. I had never received such a response from adults and children, and I liked it. I wanted this kind of attention to continue, and believe me it did. The teachers at Carylwood Elementary, Heskett Junior High, and Bedford High School will confirm it. As one teacher said, "Kim Stanley, you are a little terror."

As I established a reputation for wrongdoing at school, I also faced problems with bullies. The biggest bully in my life was a girl named Danielle. She lived next door to me and gave me the hardest time no matter what

I did. She even persuaded Ashley, my other next door neighbor, to be on her side. Ashley and I had been good friends, and we did everything together until Danielle moved to Deer Court, the street where I grew up in Bedford Heights, Ohio.

When my father learned that Danielle was bullying me, he gave me a tongue-lashing I will never forget and a promise that changed my life. He said that he was going to give me the beating of my life if he ever heard that I didn't do anything when Danielle tried to pick on me. "I don't care if you win or lose, but you better not let anyone pick on you or beat on you," he warned. "If you do, you'll have more to deal with." I took every word to heart.

The next time Danielle started to tease me about being skinny and light-skinned, I continued to walk up the street. She kept taunting me, and then I felt a rock hit me in the back. When the other kids started laughing, I decided I wasn't going to take it any more. I picked up the biggest rock I could find and turned around and threw it at her. It hit her, and after a moment of shock, she chased me until she caught me and beat me up.

I wasn't angry about losing the fight, but she was elated because she won. The rest of the way home she ridiculed me and said, "I dare you to try that again with your skinny, high-yellow self." But that didn't bother me because I was happy that I fought back against her. And guess what? After that day she never again raised a hand against me or threw a rock at me. Although she teased me verbally, she didn't attack me physically. I learned that every bully knows his limit.

THE CLASS CLOWN

When I advanced to Heskett Junior High, I became the class clown. I enjoyed making people laugh and tormenting my teachers until they wished I was not in their classrooms. My greatest fun was the classes I had with Traci, a girl who became my best friend. We were a riot. I made the jokes, and Traci would let out a scream and burst into hilarious laughter. Then I would laugh at her because she was laughing at me. We were constantly in trouble with our teachers. In fact, it became so bad that they would automatically separate us when we had classes together.

Although I felt older and more mature when I entered Bedford High School, you couldn't tell it by my sense of humor. I was still the class clown. My friendship with Traci continued strong, but we didn't have classes together like we did in junior high school. Our relationship broadened with new friends, and one of them was Eric Warren.

Eric was in my Earth Science class, and we sat next to one another at a long lab table. He enjoyed bothering me, so I would yell at him to leave me alone. However, it was not all one-sided. We would do everything in our power—from lying about each other to staging accidents that made the other person appear guilty of wrong—to get each other in trouble with our teacher, Mr. Zimmerman.

When we were in our first pre-course of biology, Mr. Zimmerman paired us off to dissect a frog. We argued about who was going to cut the frog open first, and Eric finally gave in and let me do it. After a few more playful disagreements, we began yelling at each other, and soon we were picking up each other's school things and throwing them around. Finally Mr. Zimmerman turned red in the face and called to us, "Ms. Stanley and Mr. Warren, get out of my class and go to the Principal's office.

We gathered our things and headed out the door, but we did not go to the principal's office. Instead, we walked around the school laughing and joking about teachers and how funny it was to do the things we were doing to each other. A friendship was born that day, a friendship with a bond that could not be broken. Eric and I had a lot of classes together. We became a team that argued many times over who was going to get the spotlight, and we were always able to aggravate our teachers with our behavior. Mr. Zimmerman, Ms. Meyers, Ms. Kessler, Mr. Garrison, Mr. Knox, and Ms. Ashley could all probably write a book on the headaches they suffered because of us.

Eric introduced me to two of his friends, Mark and DeJuan. Mark was hilarious, and he could do things that I still cannot explain. He used to walk on the walls at school—I mean really walk on the walls—and it made me burst into laughter. DeJuan was more settled, quiet, and subdued—the reality check our little clique needed. Of course he did have his moments when he would lose his mind like Eric, Mark, and I did on a daily basis. My friendship with these three guys made our high school years memorable. It was fun to come to school each morning.

CHAPTER 4

∽

An Unwelcome Intruder

ONE DAY I got sick in school and had to go to the nurse's office because I was coughing uncontrollably and was having a hard time breathing. The nurse frowned as she listened to my chest over and over. Finally she said, "Kim, we have to call your mother. I can't hear your breathing sounds, and your asthma is getting out of control."

The nurse called my mother and explained that she needed to take me to my pediatrician because something wasn't right. My mother came and took me to Dr.

Dorothy Early, who was seeing patients for Dr. David McArthur, my doctor, who was on vacation. Dr. Early kept listening to my chest over and over, just as the school nurse had done. Finally she told my mother that she suspected I had pneumonia and wanted me to be admitted to St. Luke's Hospital immediately.

I was scared because I had never been admitted to a hospital before, and I was afraid of needles. I could tell that my mother was scared too, but she kept reassuring me that I would be better after I took medication. She said that I wouldn't be in the hospital very long. All I wanted was for someone to tell me this was a joke, and I could go home. But nobody did.

When we arrived at the hospital, the nurse wanted to start an IV, and it was officially World War III between the nurse and me. Eventually my mother had to hold me down while they started the IV. After that was finished, the doctor ordered a chest x-ray. It showed that something was wrong, and while she was talking to my parents, Dr. Early noticed a lump on my neck. She took a pen and drew a circle around the lump. Then she felt my lymph nodes and looked at my x-ray. "I want to do a biopsy to rule out any other illness," she said.

I asked her what a biopsy was, and she explained that it is a surgery doctors use when they cannot see on the outside to find what is causing a physical problem. I reluctantly agreed because I wanted them to learn what was wrong so I could go home. Dr. Early scheduled the biopsy for the next morning. My mother spent the night with me, and my father was at home with Cynthia.

On March 13, 1987—a day I'll never forget—the nurse came to take me to surgery. I was scared and shaky as he looked at my chart and said, "Kimberley Stanley?"

My mother and I both answered him.

The nurse and the transporter transferred me to the gurney and covered me with a white sheet that smelled like it had just been taken out of the dryer. "OK, Mrs. Stanley," he said, "this is as far as you can go."

My mother stooped down to me and rubbed my forehead. "I'll be right here when you wake up. You are going to be OK, Kimberley!" She rubbed my face and kissed both my eyes softly.

I felt her mouth tremble when she kissed me, then I opened my eyes and said, "Mommy, I love you."

"Sweetheart, I love you more," she replied.

As they wheeled me out of the room and down the hallway to the elevator, I smiled at my mother and waved at her. She blew me a kiss and mouthed the words, "I love you."

Soon Dr. Early came to greet me. Wearing a mask and dressed in green, she introduced me to a Dr. Washington and assured me that she would stay with me. She held my hand as the nursing staff put a heavy mask over my face and told me to count backwards from one hundred. I remember saying, "One hundred, ninety-nine, ninety-eight..." The next thing I knew the nurse was waking me and telling me it was all over.

When I opened my eyes and looked around, I saw my mother and father. My father was sitting with his head down, but when my eyes met my mother's eyes she lit up and jumped out of the chair. She came over to my bedside and immediately kissed my forehead. "How do you feel?" she asked.

I could feel the bandages on my neck, and it felt really tight. "Is it over?" I responded.

She said, "Yes."

Then I asked if I could go home now. She replied, "Let's get better first and then we'll go home, OK?"

And I agreed.

The Conversation That Changed My Life

I'll never forget the conversation that changed my life forever. Back in my room, my mother and I met with Dr. Rhonda Sidewalls, who introduced herself as a pediatric oncologist. I didn't know what an oncologist was, but I knew the word *pediatric* meant she was a children's doctor. Talking in doctor's language, she began explaining the results of the biopsy of the lumps in my neck. Then she simply said, "Kim the results of your biopsy show us that you have Hodgkin's disease."

"Can I take some type of medicine so it will go away?" I asked.

"We're going to start your chemotherapy immediately," she replied.

"What is chemotherapy?"

When she started to explain that it was the treatment for cancer, I stopped her immediately. "What do you mean, *cancer?*"

My mother grasped my hand tighter. The doctor looked at me and asked, "Didn't you hear anything I said to you? Kim," she said, "you have cancer."

I felt like somebody had kicked me in the chest and ripped out my heart, all at the same time. My eyes immediately filled with tears. It seemed like every bad thing I had ever done flashed before my eyes, and my punishment was cancer. "Am I going to die?" I asked.

The doctor didn't say no or yes. Instead she responded, "We're going to do everything we can to help you, Kim."

I looked at my mother and her eyes were filled with tears. I wanted to swallow but I couldn't. It felt like I had a huge rock caught in my throat. I felt cold as I lay there, but I couldn't shiver, I couldn't move. Tears came streaming down my face, one after the other. "Mommy," I said, "I don't want to die."

"Sweetheart," she assured me, "I'm not going to let you die. And if you do, you're going to have to take me with you. I'm not going to let you go. I love you too much." She kissed my forehead and put my head to her chest. "Kimberley, nobody or nothing is going to take my baby from me."

As she spoke, I let go with every ounce of my strength and wailed. At that moment, my relationship with my mother took a turn that is most evident to this very day. We began to have a closeness that I can't explain or even put into words. What I feel for my mother goes way beyond words. It's the closest I'll get to God because she is indeed a gift from God. I truly treasure her, and she is one of the top reasons I'm alive today.

Preparing for the Fight

When the doctor explained the process of chemotherapy and its side effects, nothing caught my attention more than the warning that I would lose my hair. I took pride in my long, pretty, jet-black hair, and I kept seeing myself bald headed, with everyone either staring at me or laughing at me. My mother hot-combed my hair every weekend, and I was gong to lose it because of cancer. I never asked for this disease that wanted to kill me eventually, and I became even more stubborn than I was before. I dedicated myself to a personal battle against cancer. I was going to fight it with everything I had.

My life totally changed. I visualized the disease as a little red devil who was sitting on my shoulders, laughing and telling me that he was going to kill me. I even had a dream in which cancer was taunting me and saying that it was going to kill me. I grew very angry and said, "You're not going to do one thing to me."

Cancer replied, "Oh, you think so. I'm going to kill you, and there's nothing you can do about it. I'm inside of you, and I'm eating your insides up. I'm going to make you weak and tired. I have you right where I want you...dead." Then it started laughing cruelly.

I became so angry that I lunged at him. When I got my hands on him I didn't let go. I kept beating him like there was no tomorrow. I beat and beat on him until a nurse awakened me. She told me I was going to rip out my IV if I continued moving around so anxiously. Then she then asked me, "Who you were fighting in your dreams, Kim?"

"Cancer," I replied.

"Oh, I wish it was that easy," she said.

"It will be," I declared, "because I am not going to die."

She smiled at me and said, "OK, Ms. Kim, your fight starts tomorrow. Round one with chemotherapy. Kim, keep that attitude and faith, and you will win this fight."

"I will win. I promise."

She patted my hand and said "Kim, I believe you will. Don't ever give up."

My mother told me later that the doctors had found my Hodgkin's disease to be in stage four, the final stage. The prognosis showed that I had no more than eight months to live. They gave my parents two options: they could take me home and let me die in peace, or they could try to fight and start me on chemotherapy immediately. If they did the latter, it could prolong my life a couple months.

In response to this, my father broke down in tears and cried. But my mother said, "No, you're not going to let my child die. You're going to fight just like Kimberley is going to fight. You are going to fight for my child's life, or you're going to have to answer to me."

After that, everyone decided that I would receive chemotherapy. I was about to begin the hardest journey of my life: my fight with cancer.

CHAPTER 5

The Fight Begins

I WAS SCARED when I awoke on my first day of chemotherapy. In a small way—about 10 percent—I really didn't want to wake up. But 90 percent of me wanted to fight and mainly just get through the entire ordeal. I was too scared to eat any breakfast, and I just lay in my hospital bed watching the door.

When the door swung open, a nurse came in wearing a mask and gloves and pushing a pole with the medication. She looked at me and asked, "Kim Stanley?"

"Yes," I replied.

"I'm here to administer your dosage of chemotherapy," she said.

After swallowing what seemed to be a rock, I said OK and watched her push the pole over to my bedside. I thought chemotherapy would be blue- or green-colored medicine but it wasn't. It was clear and actually looked like water with very small bubbles. I was really scared, and my mother held my hand tight the whole time, especially when the nurse was looking for a vein to start the IV. When she finally had everything ready, she said. "OK Kim, let's get started."

As she released the medication into the tube that was inserted in my arm, I waited expectantly for the side effects. Nothing happened immediately, but I became very sleepy and fell asleep after about thirty minutes. When the treatment was completed, the nurse awakened me. "Kim, Kim, we're all finished. You're going to be a little groggy, and the effects won't take place until later, but you did good, sport. See you in two weeks for your next treatment."

"Thank you," I said. I went back to sleep until I awoke because my stomach felt like there were a million people running around in it. Then it happened. It seemed like everything I had ever eaten came up, first in one big gush and then two more times before I had the opportunity to take a breath.

My mother ran around the room like a chicken with her head cut off looking for towels and hitting the nurse's call button. "It has started," she yelled. "Could you please help me with Kimberley?"

I sat in my bed covered with vomit and crying because I couldn't understand what had just happened. I was scared that it was going to happen again and it did, all day, over and over again. Just when I thought it was about to end it started all over again. These were the first-day symptoms of chemotherapy, and I began to wonder if going through all this suffering was worth it. But I kept telling myself, "If I want to live, I have to endure it. Eventually it will be over and I'll be better."

As bad as the nausea and vomiting were, nothing hurt like the first time I was brushing my hair and noticed hair in my brush. I pulled it out, and as I continued to brush, the hair continued to come out. It hurt so badly that I began to cry. The more I brushed, the more hair came out, and the more I cried. My mother came to check on me and saw all the hair on the brush and in the sink. She immediately began comforting me, "It's OK, sweetheart. Your hair is going to come back. This is just happening because of the chemotherapy."

When I finally worked up enough courage to look at myself in the mirror, all I could see was the various light bald spots. "Mom," I cried, "I can't take this. Cut off the rest of my hair."

"Kimberley, are you sure?" my mother asked.

"Yes," I replied. "I can't take another moment like this again." I continued to cry and looked at my mother. "Mommy, please cut my hair. Let's just get it over now."

My mother got a pair of scissors and began cutting my remaining long locks of hair. I watched my hair fall for ten seconds and then closed my eyes until she finished cutting it short. "I have a good idea," she said. She left and came back with a designer scarf, which she tied around my head. "Look, sweetheart. You look good."

I opened my eyes. "Yeah, I do."

When I felt better, we went to the mall and shopped for scarves and baseball caps. I had scarves and baseball caps in every color you could imagine. I didn't want people to see my bald spots, so I wore both a scarf and a hat.

SUPPORT FOR THE FIGHT

My friends did not know I had cancer, and I didn't know how to tell them. Traci kept calling to see how

I was doing, and finally my mother told her I had cancer. When she came over to see me, she smiled at me. "Hi, Kim," she said softly.

"Hey, Traci," I said. When I sat up Traci noticed my scarf, and before I knew it she was sitting on the side of the bed, hugging me. I heard her sniffling, and soon we were both crying and hugging each other.

We finally stopped crying, and I broke the ice by cracking a joke. Soon we were laughing, and Traci started giving me the low-down on everybody at school. My time with Traci felt good, and it brought some life back into me. For the first time in a long time, I sat and talked and just had fun being a regular teenager.

Later that week, the news that I had cancer spread around school. My mother came to me and asked, "Kim, who's this Eric Warren?"

"This guy who is in some of my classes at school and aggravates me to the fullest. Why?"

My mother then told me that Eric's mother had called her to learn about my cancer because her son was taking it very hard. I was shocked because Eric and I had a love-hate relationship. I didn't think he cared about me that much. We were just friends, and I looked at him as my brother. I called him Buster Brown because he had a smile just like the boy pictured on the Buster Brown Shoe trademark. I truly valued our friendship, and it was genuine. It was great because I was able to get the male perspective on issues, and he was able to get the female perspective.

After I received a couple chemotherapy treatments, I was finally allowed to go back to school. However, I wasn't able to be at school very much because I was at the hospital or at home recuperating from chemotherapy most of the time. My teachers were great and worked with Vicki Marino, a tutor who was assigned to help me with schoolwork. A cute Italian lady who had the greatest smile and the warmest personality ever, Ms. Marino never pushed me. We always worked according to how I was feeling. With everyone's help, I was able to graduate with my class on time in 1989.

No one really paid much attention to my hair loss. I guess I made up for it by being the class clown. Many of the teachers didn't want to discipline a student with cancer, so I got away with a lot of things other students would not have. Chemotherapy was tough. The treatments were once a week at first and were gradually reduced to every two weeks. It was better when I had them every two weeks because I had some time to recuperate from the side effects and enjoyed a couple good days of health before I had to start the treatments all over again.

One time I had a bad episode with side effects and was out of school for a while. When I was able to return to school, I received a surprise I'll never forget. On my first day back, all my teachers and friends welcomed me back with open arms. Then the principal made an all-school announcement for all the students to come to the gym for a special pep rally. "Cool," I thought, "we don't have to stay in class." As I walked to the gym, I noticed that everyone was giving me more special hellos than normal.

I got tired of walking, and as I slowed down, Eric caught up with me and asked me if I was OK. I looked at him and said, "Don't start babying me. I'm fine, Buster Brown."

Eric and I found a seat in the bleachers and sat down together. The rally started, and the principal started talking about how the Bedford Bearcats were fighters and survivors. He said that a Bearcat is never a loser and doesn't give up in a fight, and that's what made the Bearcats different from any other school.

Eric and I were pinching and punching each other and cracking jokes about people. Suddenly we became aware that he had looked up toward me and said, "There is no greater example of a strong, courageous Bearcat than our very own Kim Stanley."

My mouth flew open. The entire school was looking at me, and everyone stood up and was clapping, shouting, and screaming. I looked at Eric and he had a big smile on his face. "This is for you girl!" he yelled. "We want you to fight cancer."

I didn't know what to do. I was shocked and so happy that the entire student body did this for me. As I looked around the gym, I started noticing that some students had signs with different sayings. The one sign that caught my eye read, "If Job can do it Kim, so can you. Fight, Kim, fight."

Tears welled up in my eyes, and I had the biggest Kool-Aid smile ever. The principal asked me to come down and share some words with the student body and faculty. Eric helped me down the bleacher staircase until we got to the gymnasium floor. As I looked around at all the cheering students, I leaned over to Eric and whispered in his ear, "What do I say?"

"You know what to say," he replied. "Consider how much you run your mouth fussing at me."

I walked to the middle of the gym where the principal was standing and stood in front of the microphone.

"I want to thank everyone for your prayers and support. No matter what, I will never forget that I'm a Bearcat...so that means I will win. How could I lose with all you guys behind me, especially Buster Brown?"

Everyone turned around and looked at Eric. Bursting into laughter, they yelled, "Buster Brown." And Eric, with a big smile on his face, started laughing.

After I gave the microphone back to the principal, he smiled and said, "Don't ever stop fighting, Kim. Always remember you're a Bedford Bearcat." He gave me a hug and I began to walk back to my seat as everyone continued to cheer. I was on cloud nine.

Some teachers gave words of encouragement for my fight against cancer, and I especially remember Mrs. Yvonne Sims. I had admired her since elementary school, where everyone wanted to be in her class. Now she was the guidance counselor at our high school, and everyone wanted to have her as their counselor. Mrs. Sims told how she had known me since elementary school and said she was very proud of me. She knew about my frequent trips to the principal's office, but she always had a smile on her face and offered encouragement to me no matter what I was doing.

The united expression of support from my friends and teachers encouraged me for my battle with the pain and sadness in the oncology section at St. Luke's Hospital every two weeks. It was something I would continue to need after the doctors gave my mother a status report about my health.

CHAPTER 6

The Decision to Persevere

ONE DAY MY mother came home from a meeting with my doctors and made an appointment for another doctor at University Hospital to see me in another week. I didn't have to go for chemotherapy the next day, and I was elated. I could go to school the remainder of the week and have fun with my fellow students and torture my teachers. I did not mind it one bit.

Months later I learned that my doctors had met with my mother to explain that I wasn't responding well enough to the chemotherapy. It didn't look like any changes had taken place, and they recommended that I stop the treatment and prepare for death. Tests showed that the cancer had spread to my left lung, and the doctors felt that time was too short to deal with the seriousness of the problem. My mother, thank God, refused to accept their recommendation. She believed I could live if we all—the doctors, the medicine and myself—would fight to beat the cancer.

We left my original doctors and consulted with the doctors at University Hospital. When they saw the seriousness of the cancer and the way it was spreading, their recommendation wasn't so far off from the first one. They said we could fight the cancer, but I needed a lung transplant. The cancer was eating my left lung so rapidly that they didn't know if I would live long enough to be the recipient of another lung. At this point, they went along with the recommendation of the first medical team.

To sum it up, both groups of doctors saw my life as a race that cancer was winning. They believed I had no chance of winning, and they felt that I should bow out gracefully. However, I have a mother who refused to let me go. She told the doctors at University Hospital, "If you won't help or fight for my daughter's life, I'll find someone who will." After we went home my mother called the Board of Medicine and asked for a recommendation of the best pediatric oncologist in our area. That's how we met Dr. Ronald Forrest, my earthly angel, who would not let go of the rope of hope and refused to let me die.

I'll never forget my first appointment with Dr. Forrest. As my mother and I were sitting in his office at the Cleveland Clinic Foundation Hospital, his nurse, Ann, came in and took my vitals. She was pleasant and had a gentle touch and the prettiest smile, exactly what I needed to help calm my fears. Then someone knocked on the door and said, "I'm here to see Kim Stanley. May I come in?"

Never before had a doctor asked to come into his office to see me. I said yes, and from outside the door came a man with an elephant nose strapped around his head. I laughed for the first time in a long time and watched as he went to my mother and shook her hand. Then he came over to me and asked, "Can I give you something I feel you need?"

Dr. Forrest pulled his elephant nose off and opened his arms and hugged me. Then, just before he was about to release, he gave me a kiss on my forehead. I was in total shock because that was the first time a doctor had touched me for anything but a medical reason. I stared at Dr. Forrest because I couldn't believe he was real.

He grabbed a chair and sat down to talk to me. "Your mother told me everything you have been through, and I have read your medical charts since the day you have been diagnosed. I read the other doctors' recommendations, and I don't need to examine you to tell you I don't like death. I plan on doing everything in my power so you and I can beat it. Kim, we're in this fight together."

Tears welled up in my eyes as Dr. Forrest continued, "Yes, the cancer has spread to your left lung. However, I feel we can slow the process down and try to save your lung with a high dose of chemotherapy. We will give it to you in the hospital because it will take three days to administer. And we can treat the side effects there."

"Am I going to lose more hair?" I asked.

He grabbed my hands and held them tightly. "Yes, but that's not bad, because I'm a great looking guy, right?"

As I agreed that he was, he rubbed the middle part of his head and said, "I'm losing mine too, and I don't have a reason like you. How do you think I feel?"

After listening to Dr. Forrest, I relaxed and felt at ease. I had finally found some help, hope, love, medication, and a doctor who had faith in God, himself, and me. Dr. Forrest then gave me the news I knew was coming: he wanted to admit me into the hospital the next day to start chemotherapy. I knew it had to start soon, because I hadn't had a treatment during the month we had visited other doctors and evaluated their recommendations.

I went home and called Traci and Eric to tell them I was starting treatment the next day and wouldn't be in school. The next morning my mother woke me up, and we resumed our routine. She got Cynthia ready for school and packed a bag for me as I got ready. She also gave my father instructions on what to do with Cynthia because she was going to spend the first night with me in the hospital. My mother was like a ping-pong ball going back and forth between Cynthia and me. She did a good job balancing her care for both of us.

GIFTS OF ENCOURAGEMENT

After I was admitted to Cleveland Clinic, I was taken to the pediatric floor, which was known as M30. I had a roommate, Julie Messiner, who had leukemia. Julie was very understanding and caring. She was jubilant and refused to let cancer get the best of her, and I learned a lot about determination from her. Unfortunately Julie's blood count became low on the second day of my first visit, and she was placed in isolation to protect her from catching an infection that would make her worse. When

I went down the hall to see her, I would have to wear a mask and stand at a distance when I spoke to her.

The pediatric floor had two counselors, Lisa and Tom. These two great, loving individuals dealt with any situation that arose. No matter how we felt, they accepted our moods and never took anything personal. They were our emotional backboards, and they were the best. Lisa stood close to Julie and me and did everything for us, from passing notes to going to the video store to rent videos. When our blood counts were good, she went to McDonald's for us so we didn't have to eat hospital food. Lisa was the best.

When we had surgeries, the doctors would allow the counselors to go beyond the doors the parents could not. Lisa would always come in early those mornings—usually six or seven o'clock—so she could go to surgery with us. She would stay with us until the anesthesiologist put us out, and she was the first person we saw when we awoke from surgery.

She especially helped us when we had treatment and were suffering from the side effects. Lisa didn't run, but stayed there with a bucket when we had to vomit. It was no big deal to her. She gave her heart and her time, and she was always there at the hospital with a game or an activity, a smile or a hug, and always words of encouragement. If we needed it, Lisa had it. And if she didn't have it, she would get it for us.

One week my blood count started out low. When it came up, I was able to transfer to a room where I had a new roommate named Lisa. She was a teenager slightly older than me and had a sense of humor I truly did love. Lisa didn't care what the world thought; she just did her own thing. She always said, "I'm not going to let some cancer ruin my party. Just deal with it."

My counselor Lisa knew what she was doing when she put my roommate Lisa and me together. My roommate Lisa became my personal hero, and she taught me to fight. As she would say, "It's cancer's job to make you die, but it's your job to prove the disease wrong and fight it. Cancer is out to kill you, Kim. Turn it around, and Kim, you can kill cancer by beating it." I admired her fighting power. She and Julie kept me going in the hospital, and my school friends Eric and Traci encouraged me when I wasn't in the hospital. No matter where I went, I had friends to help me in my battle with cancer.

One time I was suffering intense pain when I came home after a chemotherapy treatment at the hospital. As my mother was helping me out of the car, my father opened the garage door and noticed how much I was hurting. He motioned to my mother to move out his way and then bent down and picked me up. I was shocked but very grateful because I was so tired I didn't want to walk. As I laid my head on my father's chest, I smelled the fragrance of his Old English cologne and felt so safe from everything, even cancer.

My father and I had never been really close, but at that moment I felt everything I ever wanted to feel from him. When he got me to my bedroom, he put me down very gently and tenderly kissed my forehead before he let me go. It was a moment I will never forget.

CHAPTER 7

~⌒~

The Fight Continues

MY BATTLE WITH cancer robbed me of time and strength to enjoy parties and fun at the mall. However, I looked forward to personal visits from Traci and Eric when I was home and phone calls from them when I was in the hospital. Their respect and care for me never diminished, even though I suffered weight loss and lost my hair in my treatment for cancer. Instead, they came along on the ride and treated me the same as always. Traci still holds my heart as my life-long best friend.

As time passed, I grew as an individual and also as an average teenager. Meanwhile, the fight against cancer started to get better, especially the first time I went into remission. I had to go through a series of tests after every other treatment and then meet with Dr. Forrest. One day he came into the office with a big smile. "Kim, I have some very good news for you, and it's a two part-er."

As I looked at him, I thought, "If it's not that I'm cured and the cancer is gone, I really don't care what you have to say. If you're not going to tell me that I don't have to take chemotherapy anymore and my hair is going to grow back, I really don't care." As I responded to him I asked, "What is it?"

"There's a network—the Make-A-Wish Foundation—that works with children who are terminally ill," he replied. "It has you make a wish, and then it makes your wish come true. I submitted your name and diagnosis, and you qualify to have a wish granted."

I got really excited and was about to hit the ceiling, when I remembered that I couldn't have a wish granted when I take chemotherapy every two weeks. I told Dr. Forrest this, and he reminded me that the good news had two parts. He then told me that the results of my tests showed I was in remission. That meant no more chemotherapy.

As I became ecstatic, Dr. Forrest put the icing on the cake and told me he had been planning to tell me about Make-A-Wish Foundation based on my test results. And my results showed that I could do whatever I wanted to do because I was in the clear health-wise. I needed no more chemo, no needles, no tests, no medicine, nothing. I could actually get to go back being a normal teenager, no longer sick.

My mother went home and called everybody to tell them I was in remission. That afternoon the Make-A-Wish Foundation called and wanted to know my top three wishes. Out of those three, they would fulfill one. My first wish was a million dollars, and my second was a red Ferrari, which I couldn't have driven because I hadn't received my driver's license yet. And my third wish was to meet Bill Cosby and spend some time with the cast of *The Cosby Show*, my favorite show at the time.

I didn't think any of my wishes would come true, but a few days later the foundation called. My wish to meet Bill Cosby and the cast of *The Cosby Show* was going to come true. I was totally elated.

The event of a lifetime began when my mother, Cynthia, and I arrived at Cleveland Hopkins Airport early one morning. My father was going through a bad spell, so my mother said we would just go without him. "It's just us girls!" she exclaimed.

We arrived at LaGuardia Airport and saw a lady with a sign that read, Make a Wish Foundation, Kim Stanley. We walked over to her and she extended her hand to my mother. "Bettye?" she inquired

"Julie?" my mom responded.

They smiled and hugged each other and then my mother said, "This is Kim and my baby, Cynthia."

Julie greeted both of us with a hug and then asked me if I was ready. Mr. Cosby, she assured me, was ready to see me. We drove to the studio, which was located in a residential area and looked like any other building from the outside. But when we went into the building, we saw a front desk and behind it the words *The Cosby Show*. Julie spoke to the receptionist, who smiled at me and told us to have a seat.

Just then, Malcolm Jamal Warner came around the corner. I had an amazing crush on him, and I stood in complete shock and pointed at him. "Oh my, it's Theo."

He smiled and said, "Hi, how are you?" Then he rushed off to his dressing room to get ready for taping.

Then Mr. Cosby's assistant came out and said, "Hi Kim, Mr. Cosby would like to meet you."

We all walked down a long hallway to a door that read Bill Cosby. His assistant knocked and Bill Cosby yelled out, "Kim Stanley, please enter."

When the door opened, Mr. Cosby was standing there with a big smile on his face and his arms stretched wide open. My face broke into the biggest Kool-Aid smile in the world, and I started moving slowly toward him. "Is that the fastest you can go?" he asked.

"Oh no!" I exclaimed and I ran into his arms. Bill Cosby felt like a good-smelling, cologne wearing, huge, cuddly teddy bear. He kissed me on the forehead and said, "I heard what's been going on, and all I want is a promise you will never stop fighting cancer."

I looked up at him and replied, "I promise."

While he was still hugging me, he let one arm go and extended his hand to my mother. When they started shaking hands, he let me go and gave my mother a hug. "Thank you so much, Mr. Cosby, for making my daughter's wish come true," she said.

"You're more than welcome," he responded.

Then he bent down to greet Cynthia. He gave her a hug and said, "I know exactly who you are going to be paired off with." Looking at his assistant, he told her to take Cynthia to Keisha's (Keisha Knight Pulliam's) dressing room where they could play.

When we went into the studio, I was overwhelmed because everything I had seen on TV was right in my face. The house I thought they lived in was actually a stage all on one floor. On this day there was no live audience because it was rehearsal before the actual taping with a live audience. We sat down in the audience section and watched Bill Cosby, Phylicia Rashad, Tempest Bledsoe, Keisha Knight Pulliam, and Malcolm-Jamal Warner rehearse an episode I really enjoyed. I was able to see the characters as they really were, having fun with no camera and no audience.

It was amazing, a full atomic blast I will never forget. Everyone on the cast of the show came over to speak to me between takes, and I took pictures. I felt honored. It was indeed a wish come true, and for a short while I forgot I had cancer.

When I returned home, my friends asked basically the same question: "What is Bill Cosby like?" My answer was always the same: "He is great." He was and still is a wonderful individual in whom I find no faults. Bill Cosby is the greatest.

TENSE MOMENTS

I enjoyed two months of freedom from cancer before the vacation ended. The cancer came back and was again affecting the lung area. We had to step up our strategy of chemotherapy and radiation to fight, and we did. Did I like it? No, for this time the battle was even more difficult.

In one episode, the side effects of the chemotherapy took a turn for the worse, and I couldn't stop vomiting. My mother was right there to catch everything I lost and never turned up her nose or moved back because it was so disgusting. No! She stood by my side and wiped my mouth. She always had two cups, one with cold water to rinse my mouth out when I finished vomiting, and a second with mouthwash to freshen my mouth and breath.

My mother never strayed away from me through the good or the bad. After every surgery and to this day, my mother has responded to me the same way. When she comes into the room she has a big smile on her face, a kiss for my forehead, and her famous one-liner, "Hey, girlfriend."

When I was in the midst of a chemotherapy treatment one time, I started speaking as if I was a child and became unconscious. My mother rang for the nurse, who came in, looked me over, and ran to the door and yelled, "Code blue!" The doctors and nurses ran in and revived me, and I awoke from a coma days later. A piece of the tumor had broken off and wrapped itself around my windpipe. It was growing and closing my windpipe, and the doctors had to force a respiratory tube down my throat to force the windpipe open so I could breathe. Once that was down, I had numerous radiation treatments to shrink the tumor.

I knew nothing of this while it was happening. All I remember was that I was asleep. When I woke up I was in a dark cave that was neither cold or hot. It was comfortable, just the right temperature, and peaceful. There were no IVs, no needles, nothing; just absolute peace without pain, pressure, or even fear. I began to hear crying and sobbing and recognized my mother's voice. I could hear her saying, "Kim, stay with me. Don't leave me, Kim. Mommy needs you."

Then I heard another voice, "Kim, this is your decision. There is so much more that needs to be done, and only you can do it. But if you choose not, I'll understand."

"God, is that You?" I asked.

There was silence. I remembered the pain I heard in my mother's voice. I also remembered how much God loved me and I loved Him. I didn't want to let God or my mother down. So I got up and started walking toward my mother's voice. It was dark and I could not see. All I could do was listen to her voice. I kept walking, but felt as if there was no end. Finally I became tired and fell back on the wall of the cave. I began to cry and finally said, "Dear God, help me, please!"

I closed my eyes to cry, and when I opened them I saw my mother. She had a big smile on her face and said, "Kimberley, don't ever scare me like that again."

When I tried to answer her, I noticed that I couldn't because something was in my throat. My mouth had tape around it. My mother said, "Wait, Kimberley, let me get the nurse."

She ran out of the room and soon a nurse came in with a doctor following her. They both had big smiles on their faces. As the doctor examined me, I frowned and pointed to the respirator I was on. He said he would take it out, but if I had breathing complications again, they would have to put it back in.

I nodded OK. I just wanted them to pull the thing out because I wanted to breathe on my own.

Finally he said, "OK, Kim, I am going to pull this out. Don't fight it. Just go with the flow."

As he began to pull it out, a code blue signal went off for another patient in the intensive care unit. He had to leave and told the nurse to finish pulling it out. While she was pulling I begin to gag. She continued to pull, and the respirator tube hit my voice box. It wasn't painful—just uncomfortable. She told me to relax, and as I did, the tube came right out.

My throat felt raw and cold because all the cold air was flowing through my nose and throat. "Kim, how do you feel?" the nurse asked.

"Fine," I replied in what sounded like a deep frog voice.

I was shocked and my mother was shocked. However, the nurse said it was normal for my voice to sound that way because the tube had been in my throat. When the doctor came back in, he examined me and said that my voice box was red and looked sore. He asked her if she hit it with the respirator tube, and she answered yes. Then he looked at me and said that the hoarseness would go away, but my voice would be considerably different.

"What do you mean?" I asked.

He explained that my voice would be much deeper from now on because the damage to the voice box could not be repaired. At that moment, I didn't care. As long as I had a voice, I was happy.

The tumor shrank, but tests showed that the cancer was progressing. The only help they saw for me was a bone marrow transplant. I needed a donor, but first I had to go through a bone marrow biopsy. This is an extremely painful procedure of putting a needle in a bone to draw out the marrow, or what I called the juice of the bone. I was not prepared for this, as I only received a local anesthetic and some numbing medication that provided absolutely no help. I had to lie still, and all I did was scream and cry.

When it was over, I was so sore that I didn't want anyone to touch me. I didn't even want to move. I just wanted to lay in peace and let my body heal from the most traumatic experience I had ever had. Little did I know that I would have experiences much more painful down the line.

CHAPTER 8

A Welcome Break

THE BONE MARROW biopsy showed that my resistance was too low to have a bone marrow transplant, and the doctors decided to fight my cancer by increasing the dose of my chemotherapy and keeping a close eye on my progress. While this was happening, I was maturing and wasn't looking at the outcome of physical problems in such a negative way. I was able to participate in my senior class prom, and through tutoring and help from each of my teachers, I was able to graduate on time with my class: the 1989 Senior Class of Bedford High School.

Both those events couldn't have been timed better. I was in remission once again, and I was looking forward to my future. I was deeply hurt, however, when I learned that Julie and Lisa had died. I had begun fighting cancer with both of them, but they had lost their battles. It scared me, but it also gave me hope.

Julie had been in remission, but her cancer came back and she wasn't able to beat it. I'll never forget my last visit with Julie. I went to the hospital to visit M30, the floor where I spent so much time, and Lisa the counselor told me Julie was there in isolation. She wasn't doing too well, but when she heard me on the floor, she wanted to see me. I quickly agreed because I hadn't seen her in a while. Both she and I had been in remission, and didn't have to come to the hospital as much, especially since we weren't taking chemotherapy.

After I put on a gown and mask, I walked into Julie's room, planning to give her the pep talk of encouragement she had always given me. However, my heart fell to my feet, and I knew that this time was different. The smell of oxygen filled the room and Julie's bed was surrounded by a clear tent. She turned her head slowly, and when our eyes met, she smiled and slowly said, "Kim."

I smiled but I really wanted to cry. I had never seen Julie this way before. Lisa saw us looking at each other and pulled the curtain back a little. Julie reached out her hand toward me, and I quickly walked over and grabbed it. She shook her hand loose and reached up to pull my mask down. With tears in my eyes, I smiled and said, "Hi Julie. What are you doing in here?"

Julie rubbed my lips and smiled back at me. "Kim, I love you."

"I love you, too," I replied. Before I knew it, Julie fell asleep. I called her name, but she just kept on sleeping

Lisa closed the tent curtain and said, "Kim, let's go. Julie needs her rest."

As I turned to go, I looked back at my dear friend. I returned to her bedside, pulled back the curtain, and kissed Julie on the forehead.

Julie opened her eyes for a brief moment and said my name again. Then she smiled and went back to sleep.

I walked to the door, turned around and said, "She'll get better; Julie always gets better."

But one week after our visit Julie went home to be with the Lord. When I heard it, I felt like someone had kicked me in my heart. I didn't believe it, and couldn't bring myself to accept it as fact, but it was true. Julie was gone. I felt lonely because nobody understood my pain, anger, and grief, as well as my fear about cancer, like Julie did. She was gone, and I didn't know how to accept it.

My roommate Lisa lived her motto: "No matter what, don't ever give up on life...Fight till you drop." She, too, had been in remission, and she married and gave birth to a beautiful baby boy. Then, however, her cancer came back in her liver. She needed a donor, and when I came in for an appointment with Dr. Forrest, I asked his nurse Ann how Lisa was doing. Ann looked up from writing in my chart with a sad look on her face. "Kim, I'm sorry Lisa passed away. It was beautiful because her husband was right by her side."

I looked down at the floor and I couldn't swallow. A cold chill came over me, and I finally let my tears fall. As I looked back up at Ann I said, "I'm not going to let cancer kill me, because I now have two angels who are going to help me fight and be my life encouragement to never, ever give up."

Ann fought back her tears and said, "I believe you will, kiddo."

ENJOYING LIFE

Learning about the death of my friends increased my anger with cancer. I was determined not to give up, but to fight with everything I had. This resolve to live resulted in my getting back into the groove of things, and that meant my senior prom. I originally had a date whose name was Dennis. He was wholesome, cute, polite, and really shy—a cool guy. I couldn't go wrong with Dennis as a date.

However, a problem arose because Eric and DeJuan, my two best buddies, did not have dates. I was upset about this because you only have one senior prom, and I just couldn't let them miss it. I decided that they would go with me and I would have three dates instead of one. When I explained this to Dennis, he was pretty cool with it. The dates were made, and my buddies were on their way to a weekend we would all enjoy and remember for life.

I chose a dress in a magazine, but my mother said it cost too much money and hired a seamstress to make it. I picked the color fuchsia because Dennis, my original date, wore a white tuxedo with a fuchsia tie and cumberbund. DeJuan and Eric wore black tuxedos with fuchsia ties and a cumberbund. My mother rented a white limo.

Prom night was the best, and we had so much fun. Everybody looked at me as the one with three dates, but to be honest I didn't consider Eric or DeJuan a date. Dennis was my date, and Eric and DeJuan were my friends. The most hilarious thing we did was ask our driver to take us in the drive-thru line at McDonald's. I know he was happy to drop us off at the end of the night.

My next highlight after the prom was my graduation with the Bedford Senior High School Class of 1989. Our commencement was at the Front Row Theater. The girls wore white gowns and the guys wore green gowns. It was really nice. When my name was read, everybody in the theater stood on their feet and screamed and hollered, "Yeah, Kim! You did it Kim! You won!"

It brought the biggest smile to my face. I did win. I graduated with my class. When I got my diploma, I turned and looked at the crowd and held my diploma high in the air. Everybody cheered, but over all the noise I heard my father yell, "That's my girl....Yeah...Go ahead, Kim." I smiled all the way back to my seat. It was one of my most unforgettable moments.

I applied to three different colleges, and two accepted me. The first acceptance letter I received came from Kent State University in Kent, Ohio, and that is the school I chose. I was so excited because I was in remission, I had graduated from high school, and I was getting ready to start college. I had a big head, and no one could tell me anything. I just knew I was grown.

College life was great, and I wouldn't trade the experience for anything. When I started at Kent State, my roommate was a high school friend named Lolita. We stayed in Terrace Hall and had two neighbors, Cheryl and Sha, who were really cool. My hairdresser introduced me to a new friend named Traci, who was also a student at Kent State. I soon met her two friends, Stephanie and Sonya, and enjoyed being with this threesome. They were the most down to earth group of girls, who didn't judge me but were always there to support me.

One time we went to a function at the school campus center, and I noticed a tall, cute guy. When he saw that I was watching him, he came over and greeted me, "Hi, my name is Cleveland."

"Hi, I'm Kim," I replied.

"You know you got some pretty eyes," he said. "Are they really yours?"

His compliment sounded like an insult, and I answered him abruptly and rudely. However, he apologized and explained, "You never know because so many girls wear colored contacts."

I assured Cleveland that my eyes were mine and not color contacts, and after that, everything took off. Cleveland and I became inseparable; we were always on the phone, visiting each other's room, or meeting somewhere on campus. The only time we weren't together was when Cleveland decided to become a "Que dog," a member of the fraternity Omega Psi Phi. To me, Cleveland was "all that and a bag of chips"—so good looking!

The personal side of my college life was great, but the academic side was not so good. Every teacher or professor acted as if his or her class was the only class we were taking. That's why I was so glad the classes were held either Tuesday and Thursday or Monday, Wednesday, and Friday. Overall, however, I loved college life. I was learning independence and enjoying it. I especially loved being my own guardian and not having to answer to anyone. I came and went as I pleased, with no mother to tell me what I could and could not do. I was an adult.

The Cancer Returns

One morning I woke up and my chest felt like an elephant had stepped on it. I went to the school nurse, who had my medical records on file, and after she examined me she called Dr. Forrest and Dr. Little at the Cleveland Clinic. They wanted to examine me further, and they called my mother, who immediately left to come and pick me up. After I went back to my room and packed a small bag,

I called my friends to tell them I was leaving for a couple of days. I said I would be back.

My mother came and picked me up at my dorm, and we drove to the hospital where everybody and everything was waiting for me. After I had several tests, I met with Dr. Forrest, a surgeon named Dr. Timothy Richards, and my mother. I was scared because it had been a while since I was in a doctor's office with more than one doctor. When Dr. Forrest introduced Dr. Richards to my mother and me, I noticed a gentleness about him.

Ever since the nurse had called my doctors from the college, I kept thinking, "All of this for some chest pain?" Then Dr. Forrest began to explain that the cancer had returned and was raging out of control in my left lung. The left lung had collapsed and there wasn't any time for a donor. He wanted to have the left lung removed because I couldn't and wouldn't survive with such a damaged lung. The best person to perform the surgery, he said, was his dear friend Dr. Timothy Richards.

Dr. Richards began to speak to me. He kept eye contact with me and periodically he touched my hand and smiled. "We're going to make it through this," he said. He included himself in my battle against cancer, and I liked that.

"How are you going to cut me?" I asked.

He said he wasn't sure but it would either be down my back or my chest. When he asked if I had any other questions, I continued, "How soon can we do this so I can get it over with?"

Dr. Richards smiled and said we had to do it as soon as possible. That meant I would have to withdraw from school. They had me scheduled for surgery on April 18, 1991.

I gathered my things from school and said goodbye to all my friends and teachers. The hardest thing was saying goodbye to Cleveland because he didn't live anywhere near me. I had been enjoying my life in college, and I felt that I was catching up on all the fun I had missed because I was always in the hospital when I was in high school. I actually thought my battle against cancer was over.

A Significant Day

MY SURGERY WAS scheduled for 6:30 a.m. on April 18, 1991, and I checked into the hospital the day before to do all the preparatory tests. The next morning I woke up early and lay in the bed wondering if I would open my eyes again another day. "Will they make sure I'm asleep before they start to cut me open?" I wondered. As I looked around the room, I saw my mother sleeping in a chair.

The door opened slowly, and as the light peeked through, Lisa, my counselor, came in with a big smile on her face. "Good morning, Kim. How are you feeling?" she whispered.

"Scared," I whispered back. She smiled and I continued, "Lisa, are you going to go with me all the way?"

"I always do," she replied.

Lisa has always been with me for every surgery. She was the only one the doctors allowed with me in the operating room until the anesthesia had taken effect. I forgot about letting my mother sleep and yelled out "Mom, Mom! Look who's here."

My mother awakened and greeted Lisa with a hug and a kiss. "Mom," I exclaimed, "guess who's coming into surgery with me?"

"Who do you think called me?" Lisa asked.

I looked at my mother and said, "Thanks, Mommy."

She smiled, "If I can't hold her hand, I'll make sure of the next best thing; your second mother will hold your hand."

Lisa smiled at my mom and hugged her. Before long the door swung open again, and two transport drivers came in with a bed cart. "Kim Stanley," they said, "we're ready for you in surgery."

As they wheeled me down to surgery, my mother was on one side and Lisa was on the other. It was freezing cold in the basement, and the bed stopped when we got to the swinging doors of the operating room. The transport driver told my mother this was as far as she could go, and then instructed Lisa to get properly dressed in a surgical outfit and mask before we went any further.

While Lisa was dressing in her surgical attire my mother bent down and kissed my forehead. She told me that everything was going to be OK and said she would be right there when I woke up. "I love you, Kimberley. You are going to do just fine."

"OK, Mrs. Stanley," a nurse said as Lisa completed her preparations. "This is where you say good-bye."

I looked at my mother and said, "I love you, Mommy."

She replied, "I love you too, sweetheart." Then she grabbed Lisa's hand. "Take care of my baby."

Lisa promised, "I will."

I kept my eyes on my mother until the doors were shut, and then I focused on Lisa. It was cold in the surgery room, and everyone was dressed in blue surgical outfits and masks. Lisa stayed by my head while the nurse practically bathed me in Betadine solution to clean and disinfect my skin. I knew they were going to cut me down my back because that's where they were focusing their work to disinfect my skin and also because they finally positioned me on my side with my arm up and over my head.

Once I was in position, Dr. Richards came and stood in front of me. "Kim, we're ready to get started. Are you?"

"Yes," I agreed, and he turned and walked away.

Lisa came and gave me a kiss on the forehead. "You know, John Wayne lived close to thirty years with one lung," she whispered.

"Really?"

"I wouldn't lie to you, kiddo," she said.

The nurse told me to count backwards from one hundred. Looking into Lisa's beautiful blue-greenish eyes, I said, "One hundred, ninety-nine, ninety-eight, ninety-seven…" The next thing I knew, a nurse with peppermint breath was leaning over me and saying, "Kim, Kim, wake up."

As I slowly opened my eyes and began to focus my vision, I noticed that the room was warm. It wasn't the surgical room but the recovery room. When I realized that the surgery was over, I suddenly felt like an elephant was standing on my chest and my arm wasn't all there. It didn't feel right.

The nurse read my face and explained what I should do when I felt pain. She told me to push the button to receive a dose of morphine to the surgical site. Then Dr. Richards came in to explain what happened during the surgery. He said the surgery was a success, but some surprises had happened. The partially-collapsed lung was stuck on the muscle of the left arm, and he had to remove 85 percent of the muscle of the upper inner left arm to remove the lung. It was possible that my left arm would be paralyzed.

I look at him in shock, and then I understood why my arm didn't feel right. He could tell I was disturbed about this and grabbed my hand. "Kim," he said, "it's just a possibility. We don't know anything until the healing begins. We'll see what will happen in physical rehab. Your entire left arm won't be paralyzed. I believe with physical therapy you can beat this and have movement in your left arm."

Dr. Richards told me that the surgery took place in the back and said that the incision was very deep. "I closed you with staples which will be removed in a week or so, but I want you to start your breathing therapy as soon as possible. It will start teaching your right lung that it's doing all the work by itself now. I want you to start tomorrow."

"Does this man have any idea how much pain I am feeling?" I wondered. I didn't want to move, eat, and at times breathe because the pain was so bad. However, he said that my right lung had a new job to do. He wanted it to be ready to do it and strong enough to handle whatever my body threw at it.

He looked at me through his glasses and smiled. "Kim, you did well."

I smiled and held my hand out to him. He grabbed it and I said, "Thank you, Dr. Richards. Thank you."

FIGHTING WITH DEATH

After a short while the nurse came into the room and said, "Kim someone is here to see you. She has been anxiously waiting for you."

As I looked at the door, my mother came around the corner with a big smile on her face. "Hey, girlfriend, you finally woke up." She gave me a gentle kiss on my forehead and whispered, "How do you feel?"

Before I answered her, I pushed the button to receive morphine. Once it took effect I replied, "Much better now."

On the way to a regular room I became sleepy. When my nurse came into my room, she began to take my vitals and frowned a little. I was having a really hard time staying awake, and she took my vitals again. Before I could close my eyes, she ran to the door and yelled, "I'm getting ready to experience a code blue due to internal bleeding!"

I was in total fear and turned to look at my mother. Two doctors and a bunch of nurses came running and yelled, "Mrs. Stanley, please step outside." One nurse pushed my mother out of the room.

A doctor came to me and said, "Kim, you are experiencing internal bleeding. We need to insert a chest tube to stop the bleeding. This is a very painful procedure, but it needs to be done. If you want to scream, scream, but you must hold still."

They moved me onto my side and pulled my left arm back. I screamed because that's where the surgery was performed just hours ago. The doctor said, "I'm going to give you some numbing medication before I make the incision. You shouldn't feel pain because you still are a little numb from the operation."

Before he could finish the sentence, Dr. Richards came running through the door to my bedside. He grabbed my head and positioned it so he could look directly into my face. "Kim," he said, "I have to go back in to insert a chest tube. This is going to be very painful, but I need to do this so you can live. You can yell and call me whatever name you want, but just stay still."

At that moment, another doctor yelled, "Dr. Richards, now!"

Dr. Richards took his hand and closed my eyes. "Kim, keep them closed," he commanded. The next thing I felt was intense pressure and my skin being pulled away. Then I felt warm liquid flowing down my side and under me. I was crying and begging them to stop. Dr. Richards put his hand inside me and yelled at the medical team to get the rib spreaders. I never opened my eyes. I just kept crying. I was afraid to move because I thought it would kill me.

Simultaneous with the pressure and pain, I felt something very cold come inside me. My ribs had been spread apart during my surgery, and they were being spread apart again. The pain wouldn't stop, and I couldn't take it much longer. I began yelling and begging God to let me die. But Dr. Richards yelled back, "No, Kim. No!"

Finally, the chest tube was inserted, and Dr. Richards was sewing it in. When that was done, the medical team turned on the chest tube suction machine, and I finally opened my eyes. The container was quickly filling up with blood, and the pain and pressure started to alleviate itself. I began to calm down.

Dr. Richards came over to me. "Kim, I'm sorry, but we had to do this."

I didn't say anything. I wouldn't even look at Dr. Richards because I felt so betrayed. I just lay there and cried. Everyone, especially Dr. Richards, was covered in blood.

A nurse came to me and said, "Kim, is there anything I can get you?"

"My mother, and something to drink," I replied.

I closed my eyes, and before I knew it, I felt a gentle kiss on my forehead. My mother whispered, "Sweetheart, I'm so sorry."

"Mommy, that hurt so bad, I wanted to die," I cried.

"I'm so glad you didn't," she said. "Is there anything I can get for you?"

When I told her I was thirsty she went to the nurse and came back with a cup of ice and a wooden straw. The ice felt so good as it went down my throat.

MY WOUND FROM THE BATTLE

Words cannot express the intensity of the pain I experienced that day. When my mother took a break and walked around the hospital that night, I had a conversation with God as I lay in the bed.

> *God, I don't understand why I have to go through all this pain and suffering. Why do you allow me to live just to suffer? Why do you tease me with short breaks of good health and remission that just turn around in a matter days, weeks, and months into an episode of pain? Why God, why? What have I done to deserve this? Whatever I have done, please forgive me. Please give me another chance at life without pain and suffering. If not, please God take me out of all this pain and suffering. Please God, let me die. Please, God. Please!*

I fell asleep, and when I awoke, I was being transported back to my room. Of course my mother was standing there with a big smile, reassuring me that everything was going to be OK, and I didn't have to worry about anything. In a way I felt that was true. The breathing exercise and respiratory therapy began immediately. At first it was hard to breathe with one lung. I could definitely feel the difference.

Eventually, I went home and began to recover. When the staples were removed from my back, it was painful but tolerable. I was just happy to be alive. Dr. Richards told me I would have a scar, and I stood in front of the mirror and used a second mirror so I could see it. Even though it was on my back, it was long and creepy, and I looked at it often.

One day, my mother gave my scar a new identity that I carry with me to this day. She said, "The scar on your back is a wound from your long, fierce, intense battle with the devil." I also read that scars are God's signature that He is real. I wouldn't be alive today if it weren't for my scar. To this very day I remember April 18, 1991, with a smile. Yes, it was a dreadfully painful day and I almost died. But if that day had not happened and its events had not occurred the way they did, I wouldn't be here today. Thank You, Jesus!

My mother, Bettye Stanley Hines

My father, Rev. Julius L. Stanley Jr.

Mom and Dad

Mom, Dad, and me

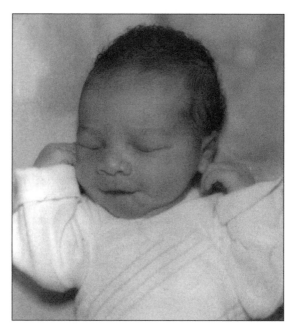

Christopher, 1998

Michelle McKnight and me

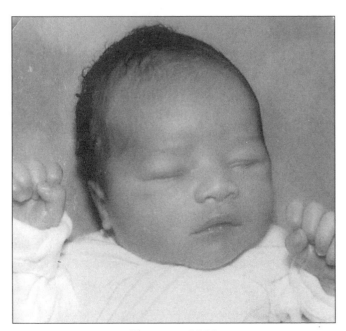

Christian, 2000

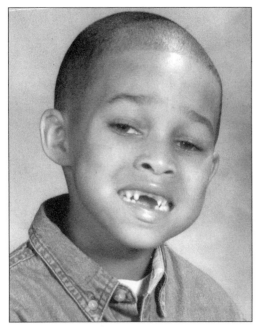

Christian, 2006

CHAPTER 10

The Beginning of a New Life

*T*HAT EXPERIENCE MADE me go back into the closet and put on all my fighting gear again. In spite of the trauma, I was still determined to live, especially since I had a taste of life. A year after my lung operation, I was much better. I worked as an operator at a clinic called University MedNet, and I also made the announcements at church on Sundays. I was doing what I loved to do— communicate. I enrolled at Kent State again, this time as a part-time commuter student.

One day a friend said, "Kim, have ever thought about making communication your major? You have the voice of a radio personality."

I took it as a joke until she told me about a broadcasting school in the area where I lived. She said I should audition to study there because it would cut down on my daily commute from Bedford Heights to Kent. Also, I would be able to concentrate on journalism more because all my classes would be related to communication.

As I thought about it, I remembered how well I had mimicked my mother when I was a child. I was commended for my work as the operator at the clinic, and I had received many compliments for the morning announcements I made at church. I decided it wouldn't hurt to get a professional opinion on my ability, so I called the Connecticut School of Broadcasting and scheduled an audition. I received a good review and was immediately offered a scholarship to attend school full time.

After discussing it with my mother, I left Kent State and enrolled in the broadcasting school. The transition from one school to another occurred without any problems. My health was fine, and the only problem I had after the surgery was exhaustion asthma.

Everything came really easy for me at broadcasting school, and I had no problems with my training in radio work. The only time I felt uncomfortable was when I was in front of a television camera. I could do it, but I wouldn't choose it. My grades ranged between As and Bs, and after I received my diploma and my operator's board license, I sent copies of my audition tape to three radio stations.

One of them was WERE, where I did my internship working as a gopher and watching the announcers broadcast live on air. But the first and only station to respond to my tape was WABQ, a gospel music radio station in Cleveland, Ohio. The program director was Daniel Walker, and he called me in for a meeting that turned out to be an interview. He had listened to my demo, and he said that I needed to work on some areas. However, he really admired my clarity, diction, and pronunciation of words. He thought that we both could do well for one another.

The station needed an evening disc jockey, and I took the part-time position. Everything went well when I came in to meet the staff and familiarize myself with the station. I met Michael, sales manager; Freda, office manager; Samantha, announcer; and Richard, announcer and production director. Richard taught me basically everything about production, and Daniel worked with me on my voice and dictation.

He told me to speak clearly, even though some people would talk about me or ridicule me, saying, "You think you're white?" He advised me, "If you can't handle it, then you need to leave." Daniel warned me that people, especially women, would try me and that men would try to conquer me sexually because I was a radio personality. However, I had to keep in mind that I am a lady and always demand respect from others. "Communication," he concluded, "is a cut-throat business where people look out only for themselves. Do you think you can handle this?"

I remembered everything I had faced over the years and thought, "If I can fight and beat a deadly disease, people are a piece of cake." "Yes," I said. "I can handle this and I will."

After one week on the air, I received a lot of compliments and praises. Many people also criticized the way I spoke and wondered if I was ashamed of being black. I didn't understand why speaking clearly meant I was ashamed of my heritage. My parents, especially my father, were very strict about the way I spoke and pronounced my words. They had a rule: no slang in the house. My mother's favorite line was, "I don't understand mumble-jumble; speak up clearly. Just open your mouth and feel your words come out the way they are supposed to come out—correctly."

As Daniel had warned, people did give me a hard time; some women thought I was stuck up and trying to be cute. And some nice-looking men came along with the main agenda of making me a sexual conquest. However, at twenty-two years old, I was very proud of my virginity and I planned to keep it that way until the right man came along.

Being on the radio was great—the beginning of a new life. I had always wanted to play gospel music, and I loved all the different parts of radio work, from production to playing the music. I had no complaints, just praises for the good time I was having in a career I loved. And the icing on the cake was meeting and interviewing famous personalities. My favorite interview was with Susan Taylor, a remarkable woman with grace and pure class. My most hilarious interview, one that made me feel very comfortable, was with Vickie Winans. And my most memorable was with Fred Hammond, who invited me backstage after his concert.

MY INTRODUCTION TO SHELDON

Although my work in radio was great, it had its difficult moments. One day I was driving to a church to make a public appearance for the station. When I made a wrong turn, another car came out of nowhere and hit the back of my jeep. Shocked and angry, I began to unfasten my seatbelt, when I looked in the rear view mirror and saw a passenger jump out of the other car. He was wearing a black hooded sweat shirt and had his hand in his front pocket.

At that very moment, another car pulled up and couldn't get past us because I was in the way. When he blew his horn and told me to move, I said, "This guy just hit me." The driver of the second vehicle yelled at the man who was walking up to my jeep and told him to get back into his car. He said he was a Cleveland Police Officer, and the man ran back to his car. The driver turned around screeching his tires and left.

I backed up my jeep to give the second car room to leave, and the driver pulled up next to me. "Young lady," he said, "you need to be more careful. You were about to get carjacked. Turn around and I'll follow you back to the main road."

I was grateful and also scared. I didn't want to do any more public appearances, but Daniel told me I had to because it was part of my job. Then I told Daniel I wouldn't go to certain parts of the city, but he again told me my job required it. He offered another suggestion, "Why don't you have your boyfriend go with you to public appearances?"

My boyfriend, Sheldon, worked for the landscaper my mother hired to care for our lawn after she and my father divorced. I first saw him when I came home from college on Fridays a few years earlier, and we smiled at each other. He was a cute guy, but I didn't think anything about it then.

We met again after Daniel fired his landscaper. When he asked Richard and me if we knew any landscapers. I told him about the one who cut my mother's yard and Richard mentioned one who cut the yards of his rental property. As it turned out, we were both talking about the same landscaper. He and his crew began cutting the grass at our radio station, and the first day they came I remembered Sheldon. All the women at the station noticed him, and one of my clients said, "Kim, he looks like the type of guys I've seen you dating. Are you going to go out with him?"

I replied, "Yeah, he's cute, but he looks like a pretty boy. I don't have time to deal with any jealous girlfriends."

Sheldon came into the radio station and politely asked to use the restroom. I gave him directions, and after he left my friend Lois said, "He's a nice looking man, Kim. I dare you to say something to him."

When I hesitated, she continued, "You're scared."

"No, I'm not," I answered. "What's to be scared of? He's just a man. It's not like he's going to do anything. What's the big deal?"

Lois pressed me. "You're scared. I bet you $20 you don't have the nerve to say something to him."

"Please," I said. "You're out of $20 when he comes back."

As Sheldon was walking down the hallway, Lois whispered, "Kim, here he comes. And you just can't say hi. It has to be something outrageous."

When he got to the front of the lobby, Sheldon thanked me. I looked at him and quipped, "You never did tell me when our wedding date was."

"Excuse me?" Sheldon asked.

"Our wedding date—the day you and I are scheduled to get married," I replied. Then I burst into laughter and said, "I'm just playing with you. My friend dared me to say something outrageous to you, and I was just joking. But what is your name?"

"Sheldon," he laughed.

"My name is—"

Sheldon cut me off. "Kim, I already know your name."

I gazed at Sheldon in amazement. He had caught me off guard. That's when the flirting began between Sheldon and me. Eventually it led to phone calls and finally our first date on July 4, 1993. That began our ongoing story of ups-and-downs and ins-and-outs.

CHAPTER 11

My Father's Final Chapter

ORKING AT WABQ gave me pure joy and a new lease on life. It also offered many fringe benefits, including free concerts, backstage passes, introducing various entertainers on stage, and entertaining format. My popularity at the radio station grew when I won various awards for favorite female religious announcer. It even got to the point where people were asking for my autograph.

But I found my greatest enjoyment in speaking engagements at various churches, where I gave my testimony of how far God had brought me and my confidence that He would lead me on. My grandmother always said, "I'm doing fine, thank the Lord." At this point in my life and career, I too was saying, "Thank You, Jesus." Everything was going great.

My relationship with Sheldon was just about perfect. As we became more serious about each other, I decided to stop seeing other guys. When someone saw me, Sheldon was always there too because we started hanging out together all the time. Things were changing for me personally, professionally, and emotionally. I felt that I needed only one more adjustment, and that was related to my independence from home. It was time to move into my own apartment.

However, my mother wasn't too happy about this decision, and it took her awhile to see that I was older and needed to be on my own. I was keeping up with my health and my doctor appointments were number one on my agenda. I had no intention of ever going back to a life of fighting cancer. I had everything under control, and now I wanted something more—my independence.

I was in love with Sheldon, and I wanted to spend every waking moment with him. When I expressed this to him, I was surprised to learn that he felt the same way. In fact, he was even more excited than I was. I finally found an apartment that was across the street from a mall—one of the main selling points for me. I moved in and lived by myself at first. Then Sheldon and I were married on October 14, 1993.

I found out that I was pregnant, but my body wasn't ready to carry a baby, so it ended in a miscarriage. That was when I decided to change my way of life to become healthier. I became a vegetarian and started drinking a lot of water.

Later, Sheldon and I got another chance to experience the great joy of being pregnant. The first two months were shaky, but OK. Once again I experienced a miscarriage, and the doctors told me that I should accept the fact that my body wasn't strong enough to carry a life because the cancer had worn it down over the years.

The word heartbroken does not adequately describe my emotions. I had been cheated, and I felt as if I were less than a woman. I had let my two unborn children down, and I had let Sheldon down. But I hurt the most because I felt as if I let down God. I felt horrible. Sheldon and I grew apart emotionally, but eventually we came back together and accepted the fact that we wouldn't have children. However, he remained prayerful and always said, "Kim, you never know what God may have in store for the future."

After I lost my second baby, I went back to work at the radio station. One day my father called and said that Cynthia had told him about the baby. "Kim," he told me, "I'm sorry to hear about the baby, but just remember that God has something in store for you. It will happen in His time, not yours."

I'll never forget those words because they brought such comfort to me. They could have been spoken by anybody, but they were spoken by my father. I loved him, even though no one could have paid me to tell him. My mother said my father and I fought so much because we were alike.

My Father's Call for Help

Three years passed, and everything was going well at the station. I was on the air one day when the receptionist came in and told me that a man called wanting to talk to me. "OK," I said. "Ask him to hold until I can put a song on. Then I'll talk to him."

I began playing a long song and answered the phone. However, the man's voice was so soft that I could barely hear him. I pulled my headset off and turned down the volume from the board so I could hear him.

"Kim," the man said, "I need some help. Can you come and see about me?"

"Who are you?" I asked.

"Kim, it's me, your father."

"Daddy?"

"Yes," he said. "I don't feel good. Kim, can you come see me when you get off work?"

His voice was full of fear. I jumped up and said, "I'm coming now, Daddy. Where are you?"

"I'm at home," he replied. "You're on the air. You can't come now. I'll wait."

"Daddy, I'll get someone to cover for me, give me directions to your house."

He gave me the directions and told me how to get into his house because he couldn't answer the door. I immediately told Daniel I had a family emergency with my father, and he gave me a replacement for the remainder of my shift. Then I called and told my mother and Sheldon to tell them where I was going.

When I got to my father's house, I hit the horn and the garage door went up. The house door was unlocked, and I went in and immediately started calling my father.

As I stood in the middle of the first floor I heard a frail, "Kim, here I am."

I ran up the stairs to the first bedroom and the sight of my father brought tears to my eyes. He looked as if he hadn't eaten in days. He was shivering because he was cold, and his pajamas were wet from sweating. I sat on the edge of his bed and said, "Daddy, I'm here. Daddy are you OK?"

He opened his eyes and started crying. "Kim," he began, "I'm so sorry for the way I treated you. Please forgive me. I need help."

I grabbed my father and pulled him close. "Daddy," I replied, "I forgave you a long time ago. And yes I'm going to help you. I love you." I kissed his cheek and held him tight.

As I glanced at his nightstand, I saw a glass of tomato juice half-full, with mold on the top. "Daddy, have you eaten?" I asked.

He looked at me and explained, "Kim, I can't even get to the bathroom."

I took his wet shirt off and found him a dry, clean shirt. Then I called 911 before calling to update Sheldon and my mother about my father's condition. When the ambulance arrived, I let them in and they prepared to transport my father to the hospital. As they were getting ready to close the ambulance door, my father yelled, "I want my daughter Kim to ride with me."

The big, strong man I had watched while I was growing up had become a sick, weak man who wanted me with him every step of the way. I got into the ambulance and held my father's hand. He kissed my hand repeatedly and continued to say over and over, "Thank you, Kim, for helping me. Thank you."

After the doctor examined my father, he told me news that shook my world and turned me upside down. My father had been diagnosed with brain cancer and had refused treatment. As a result, he had a stroke, and they didn't expect him to live three months if they didn't get him started with chemotherapy.

I was shocked, scared, and angry when I went to my father's room. "Daddy, why did you refuse chemotherapy?"

He looked at me with tears in his eyes. "I saw what it did to you. I'm not as strong as you, Kim."

"Daddy!" I exclaimed. "You should have called us."

He understood that I was speaking about me and my mother, who had remarried after her divorce from my father. "I couldn't call your mother," he replied. "She's married. And I had been so mean to you all your life. I didn't think you would give me the time of day. I'm sorry, Kim. I'm so sorry for the horrible life I made you and your mother go through."

"But Daddy," I assured him, "we have already forgiven you."

"Do you think your mother has forgiven me?" he asked.

"And who do you think taught me to forgive you?" I answered.

He smiled. "I sure do miss B.J. Is she still crazy?"

We both started to laugh and I said, "Yeah, you know that will never change. I'm going to call her."

"Oh no, don't do that. I don't think her husband would like you calling her about me."

I replied, "Before him there was you, and neither Cynthia nor I would be here if it wasn't for you. You were her first love, and neither you nor she can walk away from your first love."

He lowered his gaze in shame. "I tried walking away when I engaged in temptation with other women," he confessed. "But no matter where I went, my heart was always with B.J. You're absolutely right, Kim. You're right."

I called my mother to tell her where we were, and she left work and got Cynthia from school. When they walked into the hospital room, they both walked right past my father to me. "Where is he?" they asked.

"Mom," I answered, "You walked right past Daddy."

As she turned and looked at my father, she gasped in shock. Cynthia immediately went to the side of his bed. She was crying, and he took her in his arms and comforted her. He looked at my mother and said, "B.J, you're still looking good."

My mother was shocked and couldn't say a word. She looked at me and asked, "What happened?"

I took my mother out to the hallway and told her what the doctors had told me. "Daddy had a stroke. He was diagnosed with brain cancer some time ago, but he refused treatment." Then I told her the hardest thing: the doctors didn't give my father much time because the cancer had overtaken his body and had advanced too far to be treated. The stroke he suffered had taken a lot away from him, and they could only make him as comfortable as possible.

Tears welled up in my mother's eyes, but she took a big swallow, wiped her tears, and put a smile on her face. She walked into the room and stood at the foot of my father's bed and patted his feet. "OK, Stanley, Kimberley has filled me in and you're going to be OK. I'm here now, and I'm going to take care of you."

"You think so, BJ?" my father asked. "I really messed up this time."

"Oh, I know so," she replied. "I won't have it any other way. I need all the information from your insurance, doctors, car, home, everything, Stanley. I want everything."

My father looked at my mother and smiled. "Thank you, BJ, but what about your husband?"

"I'll deal with that matter," she answered. "Why aren't you eating your food?"

Daddy just lay in his bed and stared at my mother with the biggest smile. He realized that after all the wrong he had done—the physical abuse he had afflicted on my mother and the mean way he had treated his family—the three people he had pushed away were there to take care of him.

And that's what we did. First, my mother arranged to have an ambulance take my father home. Because he was not able to walk and he needed assistance with everything, she had my uncle re-construct his house. This made it possible for him to live downstairs and have everything accessible to him at his bedside. I came and stayed with him until my mother was able to hire an at-home health care nurse.

My Father's Parting Words

After a short while, my father's health started to get worse, and the doctors and my mother said it was time to put him in hospice care. When I told my father I was sorry about this, he looked at me and said, "It's OK, Slim. It's time to go."

Once again my mother did what she always does in times of tragedy and fear: she took control and found the Western Reserve Hospice Center in Kirtland, Ohio. We moved my father there, and he received the best care ever.

I would go and visit him after work, and one day he smiled at me when I walked into his room. After I kissed him on the forehead, I sat on his bed, and he stared at me for awhile. He looked so sad, like he was getting ready to cry, and I asked him, "What's wrong, Daddy?"

"Nothing," he replied.

"Daddy," I persisted. "Are you OK? Do you want me to get the nurse?"

After giving me a firm no, he asked me, "You know who you look like?"

"No. Who?"

"You look like your mother when she was pregnant with you."

I looked at my father and replied, "I'm not pregnant."

"Yes, you are."

"OK," I said. "If I'm pregnant you have to promise me that you'll get better so you can play with your grandchild."

He grabbed my hand. "Kim, it's a boy."

I just stared at my father because he was beginning to scare me. "Daddy, you know I can't have children."

"Yes, you can," he assured me. "Make me a promise."

"What's that?"

"Promise me that you will give him my name."

"Yeah, Daddy, I promise. But I'm telling you, I'm not pregnant."

"OK, Kim, OK," he said as he fell asleep.

I kissed his forehead again. "I love you." I knew he was sleep, but I loved to say those three words—I love you—to him now. I never said them to him before, but now I found myself saying them consistently.

As I got up to leave, my father opened his eyes and said, "I love you too, Slim." Then he went back to sleep.

That was on Friday, and I wouldn't be back until the first of the week. I had a speaking engagement at a church Sunday, and I was going to use Saturday as a preparation day. Early Sunday morning, October 5, 1997, my mother called me with the news that my father was having difficulty breathing. She was going out to see him at the hospice center and asked me to join her when I was finished with my speaking engagement that morning.

A few hours later my mother called again, and I immediately knew something was wrong by the sound of her voice. She said that my father was having problems breathing when she got to his room, and as she held him, he took one last breath. "I'm sorry, Kim. Your father has passed away."

I started to cry like I never cried before. When I hung up the phone, I looked at Sheldon and started yelling and crying at the same time. "Sheldon, my Daddy's gone."

Sheldon hugged me. "Kim, I'm sorry, but he no longer has to suffer. He's at peace."

After I called a friend and asked her to cancel my speaking engagement that morning, Sheldon and I rushed to get Cynthia and take her to the hospice center. I didn't know how I was going to tell her that Daddy had died, but my mother's husband had already told her. When she got in the car she looked like the baby Cynthia I remembered. She was so sad.

The ride to the hospice center was long and quiet, and I played songs in memory of my father. When we got there, I went straight to my father's room, where we found my mother. She was standing there with swollen, red eyes, and my father's body was still lying on the bed. With tears in my eyes, I went and picked up my father's body, hugged him, and held him in my arms. As I began to let him down, I felt air come from his mouth into my ear. I whispered back into his ear, "I love you too."

"Kim, the funeral home is here," my mother said. We experienced a cold feeling as we watched the mortician put my father in a body bag and place him in a van. Cynthia and I shared some words at his funeral, and his family and my mother's family were present at his burial. I stayed and watched the burial crew put my father's body in the grave, and then I left.

MY FATHER'S PREDICTION

Shortly after the funeral my mother called me to ask how I was doing. I said I was fine, but she told me I should go see the doctor. "You look very weak and tired," she observed. "See if he can put you on vitamins to boost your strength."

I did feel tired, and I made an appointment with the doctor. When I explained my symptoms, he told me to take a urine test. He was smiling when he came back into the room. "Kim," he said, "I see what the problem is. You're not sick, weak, or exhausted."

"What is it doctor?" I asked.

"It's called six weeks pregnant," he announced.

"That's exactly what my father told me before he died," I thought. I was pregnant just like he said I was. I still had some doubt if I was really pregnant, but the at-home pregnancy test I took confirmed that the doctor was right.

When I told my mother, she was a little scared because of the problems in my previous pregnancies. However, I kept saying, "Daddy told me, and he was positive of his prediction. I am going to give my firstborn some form of the name Julius if the baby is a girl and the actual name Julius if it's a boy." As I looked forward with hope to my future with the baby I was carrying, I determined to remember my past by giving my child my father's name.

CHAPTER 12

My Miracle

*B*EING PREGNANT WAS a great joy. I had absolutely no morning sickness, no eating or digesting problems, and everything went great. I was always talking to my baby, saying how much I loved him or her. I stayed in constant prayer for the baby's life and that I would have the knowledge and health to care for my unborn child.

Sheldon was always on his p's and q's when I needed things. I especially craved chilidogs from an ice cream eatery in Mentor, Ohio, a 35-40 minute ride from our apartment in downtown Cleveland. I drove Sheldon crazy because I always wanted a chilidog with a large lemonade. Yet, he would take those rides to and from Mentor every time.

In my fourth month of pregnancy, I went to see my grandmother in the nursing home where she lived. My mother and my uncle were also visiting her, and my mother joked about the contrast between how tiny I was and my big, pregnant stomach. Everyone was laughing, and my grandmother, whose sight had been failing, sat up on her bed. "Kimberley," she said, "come here, girl."

After I walked over to her, my grandmother rubbed my stomach and then the side of my face. A big smile came over her face, "That's a boy you're carrying."

"Grandma—?" I began.

"Yes, I know what I felt," she continued. "Girl, that's a boy you're carrying."

"Thank you, Grandma," I replied.

She told me to go home and get some rest because I seemed tired, and she also requested that I play her song on the radio the next day. I always played whatever my grandmother wanted to hear—her favorite song was "Precious Lord, Take My Hand"—and I would always dedicate everything to her. She used to sing hymns to me all the time, and that is why I knew so much about southern traditional gospel.

When I was five months pregnant, I had an ultrasound to find out the sex of the baby. Sheldon was with me, and he grabbed my hand as I lay on the table. The doctor turned on the screen so we could see the baby and then took his pen and drew a circle. He asked if we knew what that was, and we both said no. "That," he replied, "is your son's privacy."

A big grin spread over Sheldon's face. Meanwhile, I remembered how my father said I would have a boy and my grandmother told me I was carrying a boy. The ultrasound was confirming what two of the greatest loves in my life had said. It was becoming a reality.

As we talked about a name for our son, Sheldon suggested Christopher, the name of a beloved childhood friend. I loved the name mainly because of its meaning, one who gives his all to Jesus Christ. I also wanted to keep my promise to my father by giving his first grandson his name. That's how we chose the name Christopher Julius Ferguson.

I eagerly awaited Christopher's birth and looked forward to hearing his heartbeat at every doctor's appointment. It felt like he was saying, "Hi Mommy." Christopher and I had a good way of communicating to each other. He would always kick me when I did the top of the hour and gave the station name, time, and weather. I would respond by smiling and rubbing my stomach. He reacted differently to certain voices, and his favorite ones were mine, Sheldon's, and my mother's. He would always react to the gospel music I played on the air by kicking, and he loved traditional gospel ballads.

Another way Christopher communicated with me was through my food cravings—chilidogs, sweet lemonade, and vegetables. I also loved bubble gum, and Freda, the station office manager, used go to the store and get fruit cups and bubble gum for me. She was a God-send when it came to providing for my cravings. Samantha, one of the station announcers, shared some very vital information with me. Many people wanted to rub my stomach, and Samantha suggested that I be careful whom I allowed to lay hands on me.

It was joyful and exciting to go to the doctor's office and hear how my miracle baby was doing. I just knew Christopher was going to be a football player because he kicked me like crazy all the time. The doctor said he did a lot of kicking to make room because he was so long. As Christopher's birth grew nearer, the only way I could calm his kicking was to drink milk. I'm not a big fan of milk, but Sheldon is. He loves milk and drinks it constantly.

When I was in my eighth month, Sheldon told me he wanted to look at some larger apartments in the building where we lived. I agreed to this because we definitely needed more room with Christopher approaching birth. Sheldon told me he had scheduled an appointment with the leasing agent on Sunday afternoon, and when the time came, we got on the elevator to go to it. As the doors opened, Sheldon stood back to let me get out of the elevator first. I looked up and a large crowd of people—my family and friends—screamed, "Surprise!"

Everyone was clapping and laughing. When I looked back at Sheldon, he was smiling, "This is your surprise baby shower." I balled up my fist and punched him as hard as I could. He took it and laughed, and then I wobbled around the room greeting everyone and thanking them for coming. The shower was the work of my mother and my cousin Michelle. Sheldon supplied them with names and numbers, but kept me in the dark about everything. I had no clue that it was going to happen. I was truly surprised.

The next big event was Cynthia's graduation from high school. I felt bad because my father wasn't there. Cynthia was afraid that I was going to go into labor at her commencement, but I didn't. Everything went well.

And at my next appointment, the doctor told me to be ready because Christopher had been in the birthing position for a month. He said that I could go into labor at any time and advised me to be aware and keep Sheldon nearby.

A MOST PRECIOUS MOMENT

On June 13, 1998, I woke up early as usual. When I told Sheldon I was beginning to have contractions, the smile on his face was priceless. He called my mother immediately and said, "Mom; it's time. Kim's in labor."

The hospital was a fifteen-minute drive from our apartment. When we got there, my contractions were coming faster and I was becoming very irritable. Sheldon was doing all the things that he had learned in the Lamaze class, but they were not working.

Finally my mother and Cynthia arrived. They were smiling, and that was not what I wanted to see. I just wanted my little boy out of me as soon as possible. I was taking all my anger, pain, and frustration out on Sheldon, and he just kept kissing my forehead and saying yes or OK. By now I was dilated to eight centimeters and my water still hadn't broken yet. The doctor decided to break my water, and when he did Christopher decided that he was ready to make his appearance.

And that's exactly what he did. Weighing in at seven pounds and five ounces and measuring nineteen inches long, Christopher Julius Ferguson entered into the world at 4:12 p.m. on Saturday, June 13, 1998. I thought I knew what love is before, because of my relationships with my family and Sheldon. However, I did not understand its full meaning until I held that precious little boy in my arms. When he opened his eyes, looked at me, and cooed, I began crying uncontrollably. At that moment I finally learned what love is. The whole experience brought an overwhelming feeling that cannot be explained.

After I gave Christopher to the nurse and the doctor finished with me, I took a nap. When I awoke, Christopher was lying in Sheldon's arms, and Sheldon was showing him off to all the visitors who had come.

A little later when I was feeding Christopher, he opened his eyes and stared at me. I began to pray for him. I thanked God for his life, his safe delivery, and for his future. I asked God to watch over Christopher when I couldn't and to protect him from all danger and harm, evil and evil-doers. I said, "God, if anything ever happens, I pray that you will take care of Christopher if I can't."

I kissed Christopher on the forehead and told him he was my miracle baby. Christopher looked at me and reached up to put his tiny hand in my mouth. He made his famous "woo-woo" sound, and I told him how much I loved him and always would love him, no matter what.

Life was good and I had absolutely no complaints. When it was time to take Christopher home, I got him ready to go. The nurse came with a wheelchair and took Christopher and me downstairs to where Sheldon was waiting for us with the car. Sheldon took Christopher and put him in the car seat, and I got in the front seat. As Sheldon got in the car, the Babyface CD came on with the beautiful song, "The Day You Gave Me a Son." It was one of the most precious moments I've ever had.

A MOST GRIEVOUS TRAGEDY

Six weeks passed, and Traci, my girlfriend from school, had a baby boy. I wanted to see him, and we decided to get together on Monday, July 27. Sheldon and I took Christopher to church the preceding Sunday, and I planned to confirm our plans Sunday night.

Christopher was doing great, and I was so proud of him. After church we went out to dinner with Sheldon's family. I remember putting Christopher in his car seat just before we left to go home, and the next thing I knew I opened my eyes in the hospital. I do not remember anything that happened in the car accident that resulted in serious injuries to me and ended Christopher's life. I only know what I've been told and what I heard in the courtroom.

On Sunday, July 26, 1998, at 4:27 p.m., we were traveling on the freeway in our green Pathfinder. As we came off a ramp, a red Honda was behind us, speeding excessively at over one hundred miles per hour. Sheldon was in the front and I was in the backseat sitting next to Christopher when the driver of the Honda tried to pass us, but cut himself too short. He hit us from behind, and our Pathfinder rolled down a hill. I was thrown out the back window and was hit by another car, which threw me into a traffic sign before I landed on the ground. Christopher was sucked out of the car, still in his car seat.

A witness to the accident said that it looked like something caught Christopher's car seat in mid air. I prefer to say that an angel caught him and gently put him down on the ground. A passerby, who happened to be a nurse, stopped to check on me because it looked like I was dead. She checked my pulse and gave me mouth-to-mouth resuscitation. Another woman found Christopher and held and comforted him until help arrived.

Sheldon was in the front seat where his seat belt held him in. Once our Pathfinder stopped rolling over, he turned around to check on Christopher and me and saw that we were gone. He climbed out of the SUV, but a passerby held him down and told him that he was injured too badly and should wait for help. When the police arrived and examined the situation, they called an emergency helicopter to the scene to pick up Christopher and me because our injuries were so severe that we needed immediate medical attention. Sheldon was taken by ambulance to another hospital.

Christopher and I were flown to Metro Health Hospital, which helped preserve Christopher's life for a time. I had a fractured spine, and my head and the muscle nerve of my right eye were cut open. I lapsed into a coma and underwent an operation for the damage that had occurred to my brain. Christopher had a serious head trauma and wasn't given much time to live.

When my mother heard about the accident, she immediately came to the hospital. I was in the recovery room after my operation, and she passed out when she saw me unconscious and swollen. She went to Christopher, and even though he was lying peacefully on his bed, she could tell that he was having internal pain. He had a small cut above his eye.

My mother took Christopher in her arms, and he stared at her. She reassured him that he was OK and that he could take his grandfather's hand. She promised that she would take good care of his mommy. Christopher looked at my mother and smiled. Then he took his last breath and died in her arms. My mother said she held Christopher and rocked him until he got too heavy. Finally, she cried. Christopher died July 27, 1998 at 12:27 a.m.

After Christopher's funeral, my mother came to see me in the hospital where I was still in a coma. She sat next to me on the bed and began to cry. She told me that she had just buried my son and she didn't know what was going to happen to me. As she did this, I put my hand on her head and said, "Mommy." Just then I came out of my coma, the day of my son's funeral and burial.

It has been said that you lose a piece of your past when you lose a parent, and you lose a piece of your future when you lose a child. I had lost both my past— my father Rev. Julius L. Stanley—and my future—my son Christopher Julius Ferguson. Christopher was my miracle, my hope, my future, and my everything. After he passed, I had to make a decision to travel the uncertain road that lay ahead of me.

CHAPTER 13

The Road to Recovery

WHEN I CAME out of the coma, I awoke with serious injuries that still affect my eyesight and hearing today. I had amnesia, and I didn't know who I was or what had happened. I couldn't remember how to walk or drink out of a cup, and I couldn't tell when I had to go to the bathroom. I had lost 25 percent of the hearing in my right ear, and I was constantly stuttering. The vision in my right eye was very bad, and my pupil rolled around because the nerve that controls the movement of the eye was severed.

The fact that I stuttered really bothered me because my grammar and speaking capabilities had always been good. A speech therapist at the rehabilitation center worked really hard with me and encouraged me to keep talking. All my therapists told me that my situation as it was then did not have to be that way forever. Their words kept me going, especially on the many days when I wanted to give up. I didn't want to live because I felt that I had lost everything: my career, my capability to live life and function on my own, and Christopher.

My greatest struggle centered on the loss of Christopher. I felt so cheated because I couldn't remember the accident and I was in a coma when he died and was buried. As Christopher's mother, I was the one God chose to be his caregiver, and I couldn't remember whether or not I had done everything possible to protect him from harm. But above all this, I grieved because Christopher should have been in my arms in his last moments alive. I should have been comforting him and reassuring him that everything was going to be OK.

I often wondered if he looked around for me, for my last hug and kiss, for my last assurance that "Mommy loves you." However, one memory from my coma gives me peace. I was holding Christopher and rubbing the back of his head. As I nibbled on his ear and whispered how much I loved him, my father came to me and said "Slim."

When I saw him, I became very excited and rushed to show Christopher to him. I reminded him that I kept my promise and made Christopher's middle name Julius. My father smiled and looked at me with a tear in his eye. "Kim," he said, "it's time to go."

"I'm tired and I'm ready," I told my father. "I'm sorry to leave Mommy, but Cynthia can take care of her."

"No, Slim," my father said. "It's time for Christopher to come with me."

He reached down and took Christopher out of my arms, and I started screaming, "Please, Daddy, don't take my baby. Please let me come with you, Daddy. Please."

My father turned around and said, "Slim, we will be waiting for you. There's much more left for you to do. Rest assured, Christopher is with me and we will be waiting for you."

Christopher looked at me with his big eyes, smiled, and made his "woo" sound. He waved his hand at me and then laid his head on my father's shoulder as they walked away. I started crying uncontrollably. "Daddy, please come back," I said over and over again. "Daddy, please."

I opened my eyes, and I was in a hospital bed. My mother was at my bedside crying and I didn't know why. I had temporarily lost my memory.

MY TURNING POINT

Without the therapists at Heather Hill Rehabilitation Center in Chardon, Ohio, I wouldn't be the Kim I am today. While I was in rehab I moved back in with my mother, who cared for me and took me to rehab until her leave of absence from work was up. Then Eddie, my mother's neighbor, and my Uncle Sam took turns getting me to rehab. Sheldon and I had to basically start over with our relationship, and we talked on the phone every night. While we were both healing physically, we were nowhere near good emotional health. We were dealing with the greatest pain of both our lives, and this put a great strain on our relationship.

We should have been receiving spiritual counseling together, but we weren't. Sheldon was in his own world, under the devil's control and using drugs and alcohol to cope with his pain. I was in rehab seeing a psychiatrist and responding to my pain with tears and silence. For months I cried about Christopher when I went to bed and when I awoke. It hurt so badly—more than words can ever express—that was I ending and beginning another day without him.

Losing Christopher did something that cancer and death had not been able to achieve. His death ripped out a piece of my heart that can never be replaced, and it caused me to contemplate suicide. I thought, "If I can't have Christopher with me on earth, I'd rather be with him." I begged God day and night to let me die because it seemed that there was nothing left to live for. I had lost the greatest love of my life, my son Christopher. In addition, I knew the radio station wouldn't have me back the way I was stuttering. I couldn't care for myself as a functional adult, and I was miserably depressed.

I didn't want to go on. I knew death was more peaceful than my life, and that's what I wanted—peace. It also had the added attraction of getting reunited with Christopher. Being with Christopher, my father, and my grandparents was more appealing to me than life. Nothing was going right, and I felt like I was going crazy. Nobody seemed to understand the pain I felt then and still feel to this very day. It is as if one moment I was holding Christopher in my arms, and after only closing my eyes for a second, I was sitting there coping with the fact that I would never see my son again. This feeling of loss was intensified because I had and have no memory of the accident that caused his death.

It would have been perfect if Christopher could have been buried with my father, but that was not possible because he was buried in the veterans military section of the cemetery. However, my mother knew how much my grandfather and I loved each other, so she had Christopher buried on top of him. She ordered Christopher's headstone, and it was laid on November 15, my father's birthday. When we got to the cemetery, I was scared and sad. I walked to Christopher's grave and saw his headstone right under my grandfather's headstone. It read: Baby Christopher Julius Ferguson, Beloved Son, June 1998- July 1998, and had a picture of a little boy sitting on a half crescent moon.

Falling to my knees, I smiled and then cried and began to talk to Christopher. I had been crying and talking to God about Christopher before this, but I had never talked to Christopher the way I did that day at his graveside. I promised Christopher that I would make it to heaven to be with him, and that I would do everything in my power to live by God's measure so I could be with him and never, ever have to part from him.

When I came back to the car, my mother was waiting with Kleenex in hand. The song "I Will Get There" by Boys II Men, on the soundtrack for *The Prince of Egypt*, came on the radio. I cherish that song to this very day and consider it my anthem to Christopher. "I promise you, sweetheart. Mommy will get there."

After that I took on a new attitude about rehabilitation. I was determined to get better regardless of the cost, and I *did*. The radio station fired me because they needed to introduce a new permanent voice to the public, but that didn't matter. I finally went back home with Sheldon after I finished a three-month stay at rehabilitation. There I began to resume the functions of everyday living as a capable, strong adult.

I still did outpatient rehabilitation at St. Vincent Hospital three days a week, and I was able to drive there by myself because my mother encouraged me to begin driving again. After I overcame my nervous feelings, I felt comfortable driving everywhere, except on the freeway. When I started driving, I went to Christopher's grave once a week to clean his graveside and do maintenance work for it. Then I would go out for lunch and sit and talk to Christopher.

Part of my therapy was to return to everyday living. I did this by volunteering at my church, assisting Dobbie Miller with her duties as the member administrator, and answering the phone. Sheldon had a job, and I regained a lot of independence because I was alone. I had regained 90 percent of my memory, and would only forget little things. I could never be "the old Kim" again because I lost too much from the past and could never regain it, but my sense of my new self was growing.

CHAPTER 14

Another Miracle

MY MOTHER CAME to pick me up for church one Sunday. As I was getting into the car she said, "Kimberley, you look like you did when you were pregnant with Christopher. You're pregnant."

"Oh no I'm not, Mom. Please!"

"Kim," she persisted. "I'm serious. You're pregnant."

I told her that I would prove her wrong the next morning. "I will stop by my OB/GYN doctor's office, and he'll tell you I'm not pregnant."

"OK," my mother said. "But you are not going to prove me wrong."

"Yes, I am," I countered. "I'm not pregnant."

The next morning, Dr. Robert Kiwi gave me a pregnancy test. While we were waiting for the results, he asked me how I was doing and what I hoped to do in the future. When Kitty, his nurse, returned, she smiled at me and gave him the report. He looked over the test and then looked at me. "Kim," he said, "I know what's going on."

I glanced at my mother with a look that said, "You're about to be told that I'm not pregnant and I'm just picking up weight."

But Dr. Kiwi continued in his beautiful African accent, "Kim, you're eight weeks pregnant."

"What?" I said. I was in complete shock. "No way, I don't believe you."

Dr. Kiwi now had a big smile on his face. "Yes, Kim," he said. "Kitty checked everything twice. You are indeed pregnant, young lady. Congratulations!"

I couldn't believe it. I honestly thought that Christopher was my one and only chance to have a child. But God had set me down and said, "No Kim,

Christopher wasn't your only chance at a miracle. He was just the first of many miracles to come."

Yes, I felt as if I had let God down, first with my two miscarriages and then because I believed that I didn't do enough to save Christopher. I suffered depression because I didn't have any memory of the accident. All I personally knew was that I was alive and Christopher wasn't. I thought it had to be my fault because if I had done what I should have, we would both be alive or we would both be dead. Since Christopher was dead and I wasn't, I must not have done something. It was a pain beyond definition, and I felt it every day.

However, when Dr. Kiwi told me I was pregnant, I heard God speak to my soul. "Kim, you didn't fail me or disappoint me. You have tried and you did succeed in taking good care of one of my angels. I do love you, and to prove that I trust you I am giving you another of my angels for you to give my love and care."

My mother had the biggest smile on her face. "I told you," she said. "You will learn that a mother knows her child."

I couldn't wait to tell Sheldon the good news. First, however, I wanted to make sure everybody was right. When I got home, I walked to the drugstore and bought two home pregnancy tests. They both came back positive, and I called Traci to tell her.

While I was talking to Traci, Sheldon unlocked the door. "Kim," he yelled. "What did the doctor say?"

"We're pregnant!" I exclaimed.

Sheldon went crazy. "Thank you, Jesus," he screamed. The next thing I knew he was calling everyone in our address book to tell them the good news about the new bundle of joy who was on the way.

January 12, 2000, was my due date, and I was ecstatic. What better way to enter the new millennium than with a new baby, a new start, and a chance at what I thought I would never have—a new lease on life. Until I learned that I was pregnant, I didn't care if I ever opened my eyes again on this side of the Jordan. I only thought about my baby Christopher who was waiting for me on the other side. Now, however, I began to awaken every morning and speak to God and my new baby.

I wanted to choose a baby's name that would be after the three of us—Christopher, Sheldon and me—because this new precious life was the magnet to pull our family back together emotionally, mentally, and spiritually. I searched and searched until I found two choices for either a boy or a girl. If the baby was a boy, I would name him Christian, after Christopher. If the baby was a girl, I would name her Christine after Christopher, Stanley after me, and Ferguson after Sheldon.

In the fifth month of my pregnancy, I learned what my baby would be. Sheldon had to work at night and came home late, so my mother took me in for an ultrasound.

"Kim, guess what you're having?" the doctor asked me.

"What is it? A boy or a girl?" I replied.

"A boy," he answered.

My mother screamed so loudly that she scared both the doctor and me. "Oh Kimberley, this is a gift from God. I knew you were having another boy. I could tell."

As soon as possible, I went to the nearest telephone and called Sheldon. When I awoke him, I asked, "Sheldon do you want to know what you're having?"

"Come on, Kim," he answered. "What is it?"

"It's a boy!" I exclaimed.

"Yeah!" he started laughing and yelling.

A GIFT OF GREAT JOY AND LOVE

The entire pregnancy went well, and I had no problems whatsoever. My mother took me walking because she just knew I was going to have the first baby of the new millennium. I kept telling her that I wasn't due until January 12, but she said, "We are going to walk so much that little boy won't be able to wait until January 12. he's gong to make his grand entrance on January 1, 2000." I thought my mother was losing it, but I went along with it.

Sheldon was pulling away from me emotionally, and I learned that his demon—drugs—had re-entered his life and ours. I gave him an ultimatum to choose relationship with me or the drugs and his friends. With his cooperation, we would work things out. Otherwise, I would divorce him and raise the baby without him. I'll never forget how Sheldon looked at me and said, "Bye. Nobody tells me what to do."

The next day I filed for a divorce from Sheldon, and it was final in November 1999. Our lease was up in February 2000, and the judge ordered that we both stay until we had fulfilled it. We had many days of silence in that apartment because neither of us would speak to each other. However, the closer I got to my delivery date, the more Sheldon stayed around.

January 1, 2000, came and still I hadn't delivered. "I told you he wasn't coming January 1," I said to my mother and Sheldon.

"That's alright. He's coming," my mother replied.

"Yeah," I answered. "January 12."

I went to bed tired on New Year's Day and awoke early the next morning to discover that I was beginning to go into labor. Sheldon called to tell my mother, and we went to the hospital, where I started to have contractions. As with Christopher's birth, I was very irritable and in a great deal of pain. My contractions were two-and-a-half minutes long, and I was very hot.

One of the great things that happened was that Brenda Acker came to be with me. She had found Christopher after the accident and held him until the life flight helicopter came and took him and me to the hospital. Having her there made it feel as if Christopher was in the room with us.

After four hours of intense pain, Christian Stanley Ferguson was born on January 2, 2000, at 12:27 p.m. After the nurse placed him in my arms, I kissed his forehead and said, "Hello, Christian."

When he opened his beautiful light gray eyes and looked at me, I continued, "Hey, little man. It's me, Mommy."

Christian smiled at me, bringing me the joy and love I thought I would never feel again after Christopher's death. He was the most beautiful little boy I had seen since Christopher. I couldn't stop crying until I finally passed out from exhaustion and fell asleep.

When I awoke, more visitors came to see Christian and me. I was tired, but happy to be mom again. I know I never stopped being a mother, but now I had been given the opportunity to be blessed by the words, "Mommy, I love you."

When Christopher left this world, it was 12:27 a.m. Christian entered this world at 12:27 p.m. Now that's a pair of brothers working on the heart of their mother.

CHAPTER 15

The Path to Peace

THREE DAYS LATER Christian and I were released from the hospital. Shortly after we came home, I was hungry. However, because I had gone into labor early, I had not gone shopping for food at the supermarket. Sheldon went to get me something to eat, but he did not return home. I waited hours for him and ate crackers, potato chips, and toasted bread to kill my hunger. I couldn't leave the apartment because I had just come home from the hospital, and I didn't want to take Christian out.

Sheldon never showed up before I went to bed that night, and I knew exactly where he was. He was out somewhere drinking and getting high. I was so angry, and I couldn't wait for the lease to be up. I wanted to leave and get as far away as possible from Sheldon and his problems. I was too embarrassed to call anybody, even my mother, because everyone was so excited about Christian's birth. Everyone thought Sheldon was going to clean up because of our new blessing, Christian.

I was angry because I kept giving Sheldon chances, and he kept letting me down. I knew this was happening because of the devil and because I was trying to do right, especially now that Christian was here. However, it was like a knife to my heart to see that this man I loved and forgave over and over didn't care. Since he didn't care about his family, I would not care about him. I wanted nothing to do with him. I just wanted to live my life and take care of Christian and myself.

Early the next morning I awoke to the sound of the key in the front door, and Sheldon finally walked in. Christian had awakened, and I was getting ready to nurse him when Sheldon walked into the room. As he began a string of excuses for his lengthy absence, I stopped him. "Sheldon, get your things, get out, and don't ever return. Walk out now and I promise you I will never bother you for anything, and I do mean everything: child support and all financial obligations to Christian. Just get your things and walk out the door and our lives."

"No," Sheldon replied.

"Fine," I said. "I can smell you and I can tell you are drunk. I'm going to call the police and have you thrown out. Remember, I'm not married to you any longer."

I went to get the phone, but Sheldon ran and took it into the bathroom. He locked himself in the bathroom, and I demanded that he come out and give me the phone. When he refused, I told him, "If you don't, I'm going to cut your favorite Pittsburgh Steelers leather jacket."

Sheldon shrugged it off as mere talk, but I wanted to get the phone from him. I was filled with so much anger that I took a knife to that coat. When I told him I had done this, he didn't believe me. I laid the coat on the floor next to the bathroom door and told him to look and see. He saw that I had indeed cut it and came out to examine it.

Dropping the phone, he began yelling at me and saying that he ought to beat me. He jumped toward me, and as I jumped to defend myself, I accidentally stabbed him in the chest. He fell to the floor and started yelling, "Kim, you stabbed me."

I couldn't believe it. I called my mother to tell her what happened and asked her to come and get Christian so Children's Services wouldn't take him. Then I called 911, and before I knew it the police, ambulance, and my mother were there. The ambulance immediately took Sheldon away, and the police began to question me. I was arrested and taken to jail and was being charged with domestic violence. My mother told me not to make any statements until I talked to a lawyer.

As the policeman put me into the car, I felt angry toward Sheldon. I wanted my baby to be OK, and I wanted to be with him. After I was checked in and booked, I was led to the cells for women who were either waiting to be booked or waiting to go to court. As the cell door closed in my face, the loud noise made me jump and reality hit me. "Kim," I thought to myself. "You are in jail for domestic violence and you can wind up being here for awhile, maybe for years."

A Lesson in Forgiveness

This happened on a Friday, and I had to stay in jail three days and three nights before I could appear before a judge for a bail hearing on Monday morning. As it turned out, during those three days my soul was enlightened and my life turned around. As I sat and thought in the jail cell,

I begin telling God how sorry I was for all that had happened. I prayed that Sheldon was OK, and the anger I carried into the jail cell slowly disappeared.

I realized that I was in jail because I was at fault. Regardless of the events that led to it, I was responsible for the domestic violence that occurred. I thought of so many things I could have done and should have done to avoid being where I was. I was very afraid of my future, which was in the hands of the justice system. I didn't want a life behind bars without my son.

As I turned to God for help and forgiveness, He spoke to me. "Kim," He said. "I know you are in a great deal of pain, but I put you here for a reason. You are asking me to forgive you, and that is what you said you would never do for one of My own. I've heard this prayer from one of my other children, and now you understand what he feels like. He didn't mean to kill Christopher. It was truly an accident. You have asked me to forgive you, and now I'm asking you to forgive Brian Carter."

Brian had been charged with vehicular homicide and vehicular assault, and had been sentenced to two years in prison. In court I had promised Brian that I would never forgive him for killing Christopher and injuring me.

Pondering my anger, pain, and fear in light of these words, I answered, "Yes, Father, I can. God, I can't see myself sitting at the dinner table with him hugging him or ever speaking with him. But yes, I can do what I swore I would never do when I was at his sentence hearing. I can forgive Brian."

This is what I sat and thought about all day Friday, Saturday, and Sunday. I was released on Monday morning, and when I finally saw my mother, she was standing in front of her car with Christian in her arms. As soon as I got close to her, she gave him to me. Tears ran uncontrollably down my face, and I kissed him over and over as I told him how much I missed him. Then my mother hugged us both and began to cry. "We're so glad you're home," she said softly.

When I got to my mother's house, I took a nice long, hot shower. I had been denied information about Sheldon while I was in jail, but my mother told me he was in stable condition. The knife had pierced his lung, but God brought him through. I prayed for him that night.

The attorney my mother had hired told me I would have to appear before the grand jury to see if the State would receive permission to prosecute me for domestic violence. He said I was looking at a maximum sentence of eight years, and I was scared. I didn't know what to do but pray. Thanks be to God, Sheldon refused to press charges. He told them it was an accident, and the detective ruled the case an act of self-defense. The prosecution refused to press charges and all charges were dropped. Thank you, Jesus!

When I was back in my right mind, and I was no longer confused about what was going to happen to me, I called Brian's probation officer and told him that God had talked to me about forgiveness while I was in jail. I asked him to tell Brian that I forgave him, that I knew he didn't wake up on July 26, 1998, with the intention to kill anybody. I understood that it was truly an accident, and I had forgiven him. I explained that I forgave Brian mainly because I had sat where he sat after I was charged with domestic violence. Also, I realized that I cannot teach my youngest son about God and His love if I don't live and practice the unconditional love of Jesus Christ.

Brian's probation officer thanked me for calling and promised that he would relay my words to Brian at their meeting that day. Later that same week, he called and reported that Brian cried uncontrollably when he told Brian what I said. Brian was truly grateful for my forgiveness and wanted to respond to me by letter. I gave the probation officer my address so he could mail Brian's letter to me.

When I received the letter in the mail I set it on the table and stared at it for about a half hour. "What does this young man have to say to me?" I wondered. "Do I want to hear what he says to me? After all, he's the man who killed my son."

As I looked at the envelope, Christian made noise. I looked at Christian, then back at the envelope, and decided to read the letter. When I did my eyes filled with tears of peace—a peace beyond words or understanding—that comforts my soul.

CHAPTER 16

Healing and Hope

*S*HELDON AND I DECIDED to give our relationship another try. With the money I was awarded on
Christopher's behalf, I bought a house and a car. Things
were going well.

As Christopher's birthday approached, I realized that
Christian, who was almost six months old, had not been
christened yet. I met with my pastor, Reverend Otis Moss
Jr., to discuss some personal issues and receive spiritual
help. While we were talking, I expressed the need for
Christian to be christened. Pastor Moss understood my

concern, but he also knew that I needed privacy because the difficult situations in my life had been made public by the media. Since this was a matter of spiritual ministry, he said he would do the christening at church, public or private, according to the choice Sheldon and I made.

Immediately June 13, 2000, which would have been Christopher's second birthday, came to mind as the perfect date. I told Pastor Moss and said that it would have to be private because it fell on a weekday. He smiled and said, "That's fine, Kim."

Sheldon wanted Christian to be christened at his church. However, I wanted him to be christened where I knew he would be—with me at my church home, the best supportive church family anyone could have. June 13 came, and we invited only family and a few close friends to Christian's christening. My mother and her husband, Cynthia and her boyfriend, my girlfriend Traci, and Dobbie, my other personal friend, joined Sheldon and me as we brought Christian to Pastor Moss to dedicate him to the Lord.

After the christening, we went to Christopher's graveside to tell him that his birthday was very special this year because it was the day we dedicated his little brother to the Lord. I sensed peace in the air. I won't even try to describe it with words, but I will say that there has always been a peace I can see when I look at Christian and feel when I think of him.

THE GIFT OF SPIRITUAL HELP

The greatest blessing of my life has been the honor and the trust God has bestowed by making me the mother of Christian and Christopher, two precious gifts of love. As I speak about Christopher, I do not want him to regarded merely as a boy who was here and now is gone. Christopher lives in my heart. I love hearing his name, and my heart does flips of love over his memory.

Some people wonder if I will break into a million pieces if they mention Christopher, and they pretend that he never existed. However, as Christopher's mother, I carried him nine months and delivered him into this world by the grace of God. The world knew Christopher for six weeks, but I carried, loved, and nurtured my little boy miracle for nine months and six weeks. Thus, when people acted as if Christopher never existed or doesn't exist now, it angers me.

I knew I needed help to deal with the pain, anger, and confusion I felt. As I sought professional help, God sent spiritual help for my emotional problems through the person of Reverend Christine Smith. When I first started my counseling sessions with her, I was barely making it. By the time she was finished with me, I was doing flips over the mountains of life. Reverend Smith was indeed "the best." She has a spirit of sincere compassion and understanding that goes beyond what any professional could ever give me. When I met with her, it felt like God was talking to me.

My work with Reverend Smith helped me release my anger about the response others have toward Christopher's life and death. I had to be set free from the demon that constantly reminded me how others react to me and my life experiences. After that happened, everything else began to follow as it should. When I started counseling with Reverend Smith, she asked me to write a mission statement of what I hoped to accomplish through our counseling sessions. I share it below to show my emotional state in 2004.

> At this moment I see myself in the pathway of an emotional breakdown. It is not a breakdown where I would hurt myself or anyone else, but a breakdown where I need to talk to someone. My actions—the way I snap at Sheldon and emotionally block a lot of my emotional pain by putting issues on the back shelf—are showing me I need to talk.
>
> I know something is wrong, but choose not to deal with it because of my emotional pain. I believe the source of my emotional pain is the important

question, will the pain of this ever stop? I don't know the answer to it, and that is why I wonder if I did something to deserve it as a punishment.

My first issue is the death of Christopher. I feel so cheated by his death, and a small part of me feels tremendous guilt and failure because I was not there. I can't get over the pain of having Christopher in my arms one moment, then opening my eyes at his cemetery plot. I know the beginning and an end to his story, but have no middle.

It hurts so much because I love Christopher so much. He was my first child born after two miscarriages, and he was the love of my life. I gave everything I had to him emotionally, spiritually, as well as physically. But with the blink of an eye he was taken away from me with no explanation or reason. Because of this, I feel pain beyond words. I know that when it comes to Christopher I will always cry. I just want to change the way I cry. I will always shed tears because I'll never stop loving him, because I miss him so much.

I want the relationship between Sheldon and me to change and go back to what it was, and even become stronger. We have a lot of people and issues against us, but I believe our love will bring us through if and only if we ignore people with their opinions and let some friendships go! We need to go back to our dreams and resurrect some with the life they lost. We need to stop turning to others and turn to each other as we respect the decisions of others and their views on our lives.

I believe that battling these two issues will make me a better and happier individual, and both my youngest son, Christian, and I will reap the benefits of my transformation. I can't be happy and won't be happy unless my Christian is happy.

When I read this over, I can see that I have come a mighty long way. I had gone to other sources of professional counseling earlier, but it just consisted of talking repeatedly of the same issues and taking medication for depression. When the medication wore off, I still hurt and I still missed Christopher, with no idea when was it going to end. In my experience, professional counseling merely involved a man trying to help me with my pain. However, I'm a living witness that spiritual counseling helped heal my broken heart and allowed God to repair my wounded soul.

Complete healing won't come until I reach heaven. However, until then, God has put a band-aid on my heart and soul. It will come off when I reach heaven, but now I am doing just fine. I'm going to make it to heaven—first because I love God, and that's where I want to be eternally, and because I promised Christopher that I would get there through my faith in Jesus. There are a few promises we can make and keep, but this is one I promised my baby. I dedicated my life to God and told Him that I'll be just fine if my reward is a place in heaven with Him and my two boys.

CHAPTER 17

My Thank Offering

s I look back over my life, I can truly say I wouldn't be here today if it had not been for the grace and mercy of the Lord Jesus Christ. I do not understand why I have had so many trials and tribulations. I truly believe that everything has happened for a reason, and God will show that reason to me when I get to heaven. Although I have been asking God for an explanation for a long time, I am learning instead to just thank Him for bringing me through all the pain and suffering I have experienced.

When I think of my father, I remember how I wanted him to love me because I loved him. He treated me wrongly for many years, but one day he called me unexpectedly and gave me words of comfort when I was heartbroken about losing two unborn children. By making the call, his actions showed that he did love me.

My father expressed respect for me as an adult when he called me and asked me to help him near the end of his life. I could have refused him because of the way he treated my mother and me. But I thank God I didn't, because I received what I always wanted—my father's love—during the last three months of his life. This erased all the pain of the past, and although I have not forgotten it, I have forgiven him because my mother raised me to be a loving, spiritual woman.

God blessed me with an angel—my mother—who has held my hand and helped me through all my life experiences. My mother has taught me how to be a mother. She has shown me that the responsibility and love of a mother do not stop when a child becomes an adult. It continues even until death, no matter how old the child is. My mother is my best friend. She is always there for me and always honest. She is always trying to protect me from the world, even though she knows she can't.

I learned respect from my mother by watching her respect my grandmother, Ida Fisher. I watched my mother give her life to help save my life, and I saw her sacrifice so my sister and I could have the very best. Every time I awakened from surgery, the first face I saw was my mother's. When I had questions, she was always ready to answer them, even if she felt uncomfortable doing it.

Although I have watched my mother express love all my life, nothing I saw compares to the love she has and shares for Christopher and Christian. To this very day, she keeps Christopher's memory alive and does not ignore his existence. Her love for Christian can be seen and felt, but it cannot be adequately described with words. She gives so much of herself to Christian, and Christian loves his Granny with all his heart. I know that if I couldn't physically be here to love and care for Christian, I would still be present emotionally through the love of my mother.

Sheldon and I have been together over ten years, and I thank the Lord for it. We have gone through a lot, and our problems have sometimes separated us. However, our love for each other has always brought us back to each other. While I do hope and pray for more changes and upgrades in our relationship, I'm grateful for the time we have had together. I have grown and learned a great deal.

We aren't the picture-perfect postcard of a good relationship, but we are a small part of the definition of love. We have come to where we are today because of God and our love. Through it all, the two greatest and best things we have ever shared are Christopher and Christian. And when we reach heaven we'll get to meet the two unborn children we lost.

CHRISTOPHER AND CHRISTIAN

Christopher helped me discover something I never knew was in me—the gift of unconditional, perfect love. I knew it existed, but I didn't realize its power until I experienced his development into the child who has become one of the loves of my life. I will never forget the way Christopher reacted to my voice when I spoke to him while I was pregnant. The way he communicated with me while he grew within me and the first time our eyes met on the day of his birth stirred within me a commitment to protect my baby boy from any source of harm.

I can't begin to describe the love I have for my baby boy Christopher, but I do know that it will never die. I miss his touch, his smell, the way he looked at me, and his smile. When I had my sweet Christopher, it was as if no one else existed but him. I love to hear his name, and I love to say it. I don't know why God only gave

Christopher a short stay on earth, but I know He will tell me when I get to heaven.

Yes, Christopher was indeed the perfect angel who completed his life's assignment on Earth in six weeks. I look forward to the day when I enter heaven's gate and my baby will be standing there with a big smile. He'll welcome me and say, "You kept your promise. I've been waiting for you. Welcome home, Mom!"

A big part of my depression was the fact that I thought Christopher was my one and only chance at being a mother. When I lost him, I thought I had lost my chance to experience the gift of love that only a mother feels when she carries and gives birth to a child. I felt that I had failed God because I couldn't protect Christopher, and I continued to feel like a failure until the day I learned that I was pregnant with Christian.

Christian became my angel of life. The love I thought was gone was awakened when his life began within me, and his birth brought everything I thought was dead back to life. My love for Christian is the love of a mother who has truly endured and has been blessed with a child at the end of a tedious, devil-sent trial. He is the love of my life.

I know my name is Kim Stanley, but nothing brings greater joy to my heart than to hear Christian call me

"Mommy." I have great hopes for his future, and I'll be with him every step of the way, whatever road he decides to travel. My love won't stop when Christian becomes a man, and I always tell him, "Mommy doesn't care how old you are, fifty-three or even eighty-three. No matter how old you are, you'll always be Mommy's baby in my heart." When I say this, Christian smiles back, and I know that he knows his mommy loves him with all her heart.

THE LIGHT OF MY WORLD

Still, my love for Christian or anyone else cannot compare to the first love of my heart, my life, and my soul—my Lord and Savior Jesus Christ. God has brought me through so much, and I could never adequately describe His love and care for me. This book is one way I can say thank you as an expression of my love for Christ.

The movie *The Passion of the Christ* is the best portrayal I have ever seen of God's love for us. The part that left a lasting impression on me was the scene when Jesus died on the cross and one single tear fell from God to the earth. By this act of love, God made it possible for mankind to change and took the devil out of victory forever.

The devil has made a lot of points in the game of life, especially in my life. In fact, sometimes he has been in the lead. However, I make a promise to anyone who reads this book or hears my testimony that the Lord Jesus will be the Victor in my life. I can't speak for anyone else, but the Lord Jesus has my soul. The devil may get some points and take the lead at times, but the victory in my life belongs to my Lord and Savior, Jesus Christ.

I thank the Lord every night and every morning because I should have been dead a long time ago. Instead, I'm living proof that when life is at its worst and we can't see Him, hear Him, or feel Him, God is at His best. We don't know when the race will end. At times we might have a rest before the devil tries to put another stumbling block in our path. However, we know that throughout the race, God will give us all the water breaks we need. Just as water replenishes the body with strength to run, God's Living Water will replenish and nurture our body, soul, and mind.

We must not give up because God is going to bring us through. We can hold on to our faith and the fact that God loves us, regardless of the problems and obstacles the devil puts in our path. My life has been a dark, arduous journey. The only reason I'm here today is that a light—Jesus Christ, the Light of the World—has guided me through every day. We may not have the strength to go on, but we can look to heaven and pray what I've been saying for over thirty years.

God I don't understand. I feel this is unfair, and I just want to come home because I'm tired. But God, I love you. Thank You, Lord Jesus!

CHAPTER 18

God Isn't Finished With Me Yet

*W*HILE I WAS waiting for this book to be edited, I faced another serious health issue. During my yearly physical in January, 2006, my doctor, Dr. Carla Harwell, found a lump right under my jaw line on the side of my neck. She sent me to Dr. Pierre Lavertu, an ENT Specialist who had previously removed my thyroid and another cyst from my throat.

Dr. Lavertu was unable to help me with non-surgical treatment, so he decided to remove the tumor. If the tumor was benign, he would stitch me up and that would be all. If it was malignant, he would remove all the lymph modes from the right side of my neck, which would require a three-to-four day stay in the hospital. I was fine with this because I trusted Dr. Lavertu whole-heartedly, and we scheduled the surgery for Monday, July 31.

Because I knew I would be out of commission a week or two after the surgery, I went shopping for needed supplies and made sure all the bills were paid. I also met with Pastor Moss and gave him a copy of this book. He prayed for my surgery, and something about his prayer brought such peace to my soul.

On Sunday I took Christian to my mother's house because she had agreed to watch him the week after my surgery. Before I left to go home, Christian said, "Mommy, I prayed to God, and you are going to be just fine."

"I love you sweetheart," I assured him as we gave each other a big hug and a kiss. Then I went home to pray and relax.

The next day I checked into the hospital at 7:20 a.m. Sheldon, Cynthia, and my cousin Michelle sat and waited with me before the surgery. I didn't want Christian at the hospital, so my mother was going to take him to the zoo and the beach. When I woke up in recovery, I received the great news that the tumor was not cancerous and

I was OK to go home in an hour. I was given home instructions and a prescription for pain, and soon the nurse was taking me in a wheelchair to the pickup area where Sheldon was waiting to take me home.

As we traveled home, I told Sheldon that I was experiencing some pain. We stopped at the pharmacy to have my prescription filled, and once we got home I opened the bottle. "These pills look like horse pills," I said. "I'm going to cut this in half because it's too big to swallow. My throat is already swollen from the surgery."

Even though it was only half a pill, it got stuck in my throat, and I took another gulp of water to push it down. However, something didn't feel right, and I put my hand up to my neck. When I looked at my hand, it was covered in blood. I tried to call Sheldon, but no sound came out of my mouth. I also noticed that I was having a hard time breathing, and I was really scared.

To get Sheldon's attention, I started slamming the cabinet doors really hard. He ran into the kitchen and when he saw me, the look on his face confirmed that something was wrong. "What happened, Kim?" he asked.

All I could do was show him the bottle of pills. He put a towel on my neck and quickly called 911. Although it seemed like forever, the ambulance arrived within minutes. Since I could not talk, I wrote the answers to the questions of the paramedics on their clipboard. They thought I might be having an allergic reaction to the pain medication, so they started an IV and rushed me to the Richmond Heights University Hospital Emergency Room.

They wouldn't let me lie down, and I didn't want to anyway because I couldn't breathe. Once the medication kicked in and an oxygen mask was put on my face, however, breathing became a little easier. The medical team started working on me the instant I arrived at the hospital and decided to suck out some of the blood. This meant they had to cut the stitches out and reopen the wound where I had surgery that morning.

Christine, one of the kindest nurses on the staff, looked me straight in the face and explained everything they were doing. I couldn't move, breathe or talk, and I just lay there like a zombie as they began to cut the stitches loose. Multiple people were working on me at the same time. When I felt the wound open after all the stitches were removed, I looked to the heaven and said, "I'm getting ready to die. Oh my God."

Paralyzed by fear, I opened my eyes to see what was happening and looked down at my feet. Cynthia was standing in the doorway and looking at me with such fear and shock. "Oh my," I said to myself, "this is the last time Cynthia will see me alive."

I blinked, and suddenly I saw my father standing behind Cynthia. I couldn't believe it! Daddy had come to get me. I knew then that I was going to die.

However, my father looked at me and smiled. "Not yet, Slim. It's not time to go; not yet."

Immediately I remembered when I saw my father just before I came out of the coma that resulted from the accident, when he came to me and took Christopher with him. I remembered his promise that they would wait for me. And when I didn't see Christopher with my father, my mind jumped to Christian.

That's when my heart got the spark of life I needed to continue. I begin praying to God as loud as my soul could scream. "Please God, don't take me away from my baby. I can't leave my baby. Please God, no. I want to live. I need to live, I have to live, I must live. I can't do this to my baby. God, he's only six years old. Please, dear Jesus, don't take me away from my baby." Over and over, I kept praying that God would allow me to live.

Christine bent down and looked into my face. "Kim, Life Flight is here to fly you back to University Hospital. Dr. Lavertu wants you back with him."

I nodded my head. A man and a woman dressed in blue came to me and introduced themselves as the paramedics who were going to fly with me to University Hospital. Christine came over to me one more time and squeezed my hand, "OK, Kim, this is where we depart. You hang in there."

MY DESPERATE PRAYER IS ANSWERED

Breathing became easier after the medical team cut the stitches and sucked some of the excess blood from my neck. I also had an oxygen mask on me, and that made my breathing better than it was before. The paramedics pushed me outside to the helicopter. The door closed, and as the helicopter began to rise, I looked out the window at the clouds. "God." I prayed one more time, "I don't want to leave this world, especially my baby Christian. I will do and go through whatever I have to, just don't take me away from him yet."

The helicopter ride took four minutes, and before I knew it, I felt a thump. The paramedics quickly pushed me into University Hospital, and soon Dr. Lavertu was looking into my face. "I don't know what happened," he said, "but I'm going to find out. You are very swollen, Kim, and you have lost some blood. This is an emergency, so I don't have time to put you out. I'm sorry, but

I need to go back in and find what's wrong so I can fix it. I'm not losing you."

As I stared at Dr. Lavertu, I was overcome with fear. "Oh God, what's going on?" I wondered. I couldn't move or talk; all I could do was lie on the bed and hope the doctors would do what needed to be done. "God," I prayed, "please don't let me feel everything."

I started to cry, hoping that my tears would communicate my apprehension and my desperate need for Dr. Lavertu to take care of me. He gently touched me and said, "I'm sorry, Kim," and lifted the scalpel.

The next thing I knew I was opening my eyes. A nurse came and told me that I was in the intensive care unit and had a breathing tube in my nose. Then my mother came in and wiped my forehead. She greeted me as she always did: "Hey, girlfriend."

My mother assured me that Christian was fine. He had been feasting on pizza in the hospital cafeteria, and now my cousin Michelle and her daughter Tottie were watching him in the waiting area. My mother had been coming to see me numerous times, and Christian didn't like it when she stayed away from him a long time. Communicating by paper and pen, I told her, "Go back to Christian. I'll be all right."

After a while, my family members began to come and see me. Words can't adequately express what I felt when Pastor Moss walked in and took my hand. "Kim," he said, "let's have a word of prayer."

When he finished praying, he smiled at me, patted my hand, and slowly walked away. I felt relieved. A peace that went beyond human understanding assured my soul, mind, and body that everything was going to be OK.

While I was in surgery, the doctors sewed a drainage tube into my neck to catch the drainage from the incision. I spent three days in the intensive care unit, and on the second day they inserted a feeding tube in my nose. Thus, I was equipped with a breathing tube in one nostril, a feeding tube in the other, and a drainage tube in my neck. I didn't want to be moved or touched. Finally, on the third day at 11:30 p.m., I was transferred from intensive care to a private room on one of the floors. That meant the tubes from my nose were removed. Thank You, Jesus!

Two days later the doctor gave me the good news that they were going to remove the drainage tube from my neck the next morning. Then they wanted to watch me for four hours and promised that I could go home if I didn't have any problems. I woke up at 5:00 a.m., and as

I waited for the doctor, I talked to God and told him how grateful I was to be alive.

At 6:20 a.m. the doctors came in. As one of them cut the stitches that held the tube in my neck, the other one talked me through the entire procedure. Finally there was a little tug on my neck, and the doctor said, "Kim, it's out."

That is when I started to breathe again. The doctors wanted me to eat so they could be sure all the internal swelling in my neck had gone down. My mother came to pick me up, and we walked to the hospital cafeteria to eat lunch. It was the first time since my hospitalization that I had walked from one area to another, and it felt so good to be alive.

Mommy and I went back to the room and began to watch a movie together. The doctors came back and asked a few questions as they examined my neck. Then they gave me the OK to go home. I was elated!

MY LIFE IS RESTORED

When we were about to leave, the nurse asked if I would I like a wheelchair, and I answered with an emphatic no! My mother said that she had to park in the parking garage that morning and it was quite a distance. She wondered out loud if I should ride in the wheelchair.

Looking at my mother, I replied, "I'll be OK. I want to walk. I've been on my back for the past week and I want to walk. I need to walk."

We got on the elevator, and when stepped off onto the first floor, I realized that I was leaving the place I thought would be the final stop of my life. I was brought in by helicopter for emergency surgery, and I spent three days in intensive care. I heard the words "code blue" numerous times, and always wondered if that was going to be me. At first I was pushed down the hallway on a gurney and then improved so I could walk down the hallway with my own strength. Now I was walking out of the hospital thankful that I was alive.

I came close to death in my fight with cancer and in the car accident that took Christopher's life. But this time I really saw the power of God because I was awake in the surgery. I could see, hear, and feel everything that was going on. It was an ordeal, yet I was still here! My health stabilized to fair condition, and I was here to love my son and care for him.

On Monday, my son Christian said he wanted a McDonald's lunch. McDonald's is right up the street from us, and I insisted that I would go get his lunch by myself. When I came back, Juanita Bynum was singing "Above All Else" on my CD player. I parked the car and cried to God, "Here I am, one week from the day I thought I was going to meet death. I couldn't breathe for myself, I couldn't feed myself, and I had to endure the worst pain ever. That was just a matter of days ago, and here I am now walking, talking, and yes, driving."

What really touched me was the fact that I was able to care for my son Christian. I did something that just a few days ago I thought I would never be able to do. I cried and cried, "Thank You, God! Thank you! It's good to be alive! I truly am grateful for life and all You have to offer us, if only we believe."

The day of relief came when I went to have the stitches removed from my neck. My mother and Christian came with me and asked if they could come into Dr. Lavertu's office with me.

"Sure, come on in," he said.

My mother and Christian watched as Dr. Lavertu cut the stitches away. "Are you ready?" he asked me.

"Yes," I replied. "I've been ready."

My mother covered Christian's eyes and then her eyes, but Christian pulled my mother's hands away and said, "No, Granny, I want to watch."

Dr. Lavertu pulled the stitches out of my neck, and I felt a great release of pressure. As I looked at the incisions in the mirror, he told me it looked worse than what it was because the stitches had just been pulled out. "The swelling will eventually go down," he explained, "but unfortunately there will be a scar."

"A scar?" I replied. "I always wanted a tattoo, and now I have one that God gave me. I have a heavenly tattoo, a tattoo that shows God restored life to me."

My scars offer me a daily reminder of the goodness, grace, and healing that God continues to work in me. It is a testimony that He is not finished with me yet. I cannot be sure of what the next chapter in my life's story may hold, but I thank the Lord that He'll be with me every step of the journey.

To Contact the Author

cj613cs12@sbcglobal.net or (216) 978-2832